Words of Praise from Salespeople, Managers, Executives and Authors

"David's book offers not only some quality insights into the professional sales process, but more importantly has a focus on activity management and sales planning."
— Kelcey Lehrich, Director of Corporate Sales and Franchising for Teresa's Pizza of Cleveland, Ohio

"If you want to be an effective salesperson this book will help you with that. It's a great book for anyone without a sales background and for experienced salespeople alike. It gets back to basics by describing a tried and true sales process that works!"
— Jessica Medina, Recruiter, CA

"David Masover's book, Mastering Your Sales Process, effectively teaches the entire business development process from prospecting to customer implementation and will inspire the seasoned veteran as well as the rookie salesperson in search for 'the complete modern sales process instruction manual.' Few sales training books provide the breadth as well as depth found in this one."
— Bud Suse, Author of "Closing the Whales: The Anatomy of Major Deals—A Proven Process for Complex, High Tech Sales Campaigns"

"This book spells-out a straightforward, powerful process that will help you succeed in almost any sales situation. One of its many strengths is that David makes it easy for you to know just when to move on to each next point of the process—a key element many other books lack."
— Shawn A. Greene, Author of "I'd Rather Have a Root Canal Than do Cold Calling!"

"Having been in sales for 30 years, I can tell you that David is right on in his approach. David has identified the crucial key to success in this industry—following a system. There is much financial opportunity in sales, over a wide spectrum of industries. This book outlines a process for you to follow toward that success. Many salespeople think it's their industry that isn't working and they spend their days looking for that perfect opportunity. Many of them are very talented people. Focusing on a proven process gives you the comfort in knowing you can succeed if you only follow it. I highly recommend David Masover's book to any salesperson who is dedicated to succeeding."
— Joe Pipkin, Senior Freight Consultant at InXpress,
  Memphis, TN

"A great resource for both beginners and experienced sales professionals. David provides a new take on all the relevant sales concepts, in a concise volume with clear explanations and examples to illustrate the concepts."
— John Cantwell, Managing Director, Dramatrix Hungary

"Mastering Your Sales Process should be the first sales training book you read and use after learning the basic steps of your own sales methodology. What David has to offer is the roadmap to repeat success. Once you implement his suggestions, you will be able put your sales process on 'cruise control,' never wonder what you should do next, and consistently meet your goals without bumpy 'up and down' sales cycles."
— Kevin Nicholas O'Neil, M.S., O'Neil Advocacy Group

"Mastering Your Sales Process is a virtual blueprint for sales success. It is a must- read for anyone new in the field of sales or experienced reps who want to improve their results and earning potential. If you're in sales management, this book clearly lays out new sales weapons to add to your arsenal that you can put into action today."
— Matthew Lynch, Russell Europe, Country Manager,
  Scandinavia, Central and Eastern Europe

"As a dedicated sales development company, we were pleased to be able to review the book entitled Mastering Your Sales Process. The pragmatic and systematic approach demystifies the black art that sales that is often thought to be. Recommended for anyone that wants to get into sales through seasoned professional salespeople."
— Mark Jacobs, Director of The Mdina Partnership, Ltd.
  www.mdina.co.uk

"If it was not protected by copyright, I would have suggested that David call his book 'Sales Process for Dummies.' Even the most experienced, talented salesperson has something to learn from this book, as there are many 'dummy' salespeople out there at all levels of experience! While the book can be described as simple, straight-forward, precise, very well documented and full of good examples, I would rather highlight the book's practicality and very useful exercises that I recommend every reader should spend some time on."

— Emanuele Massimo, Technical industry sales
& marketing professional

David Masover

MASTERING
YOUR SALES PROCESS

How to Create a
Winning Sales Process
for You, Your Boss, and Your Prospects

Foreword by Jerry McLaughlin

ISBN: 1-4392-6895-9

ISBN-13: 9781439268957

Professional Dedication

Dedicated to those sales professionals who are trying to get better at the art of selling, make more money in the process, and still have time left for the rest of their lives!

Personal Dedication

To Kata, Ben and Elie—my collective everything!

ACKNOWLEDGEMENTS

Over the course of my twenty-plus year sales career, there have been too many influences to list. I have worked hard to learn where I could and have been fortunate to have some truly inspirational people to learn from along the way.

Some of the more influential professional mentors include: Jerry McLaughlin, David Sipes, Bob Noakes, Dave Kurlan, Rush Burkhart, Ray Decker, Larry Seidman, Jerry Gleicher, John Huffman and many more. Thank you all for taking a personal interest in helping me to learn and grow, and for the time you spent sharing your wisdom with me.

I also have read what feels like a few thousand books on sales—far too many to list. Having now written this book, I can appreciate both the joy of compiling one's philosophy and tactics for public consumption and the hard work that goes into doing so. As such, thank you, Brian Tracy, Stephen Covey, Stephan Schiffman, Jeffrey Gitomer, Tom Peters, Dave Kurlan, and dozens more, whose work has both influenced and inspired me.

Finally, salespeople need to overcome challenges as a part of their work; the resulting frustrations and celebrations can sometimes spill over into the rest of life. Accordingly, I have immeasurable gratitude for my family, bearers of the brunt of all I have to offer—good, bad, and ugly.

For my mother, Bonnie, may you rest in peace. I am sorry that you had to leave us so soon. There are no words to capture my feelings other than I love you and thank you. I wish you were here to see me all grown up now.

To my father, Jerry, who is always there to listen and "cogitate" with me, and his wife Lee, the effective grandmother of my children; you are always full of ideas and always ready to help.

To my siblings, Steve and Laurie, who could not be more different from me with respect to profession, but who politely listen anyway.

To my young children, Ben and Elie, for pretending to understand when "Apa" had to go to another business meeting in Hong Kong or America; when I was just plain grouchy; when I was hammering at the computer— or sometimes all of the above.

Last—and on the opposite side of the spectrum from least—I thank my wife, Kata. In spite of all of the reasons I have given you to pull your hair out (or mine), you are always there to support me with more love and more brains than I ever thought one person could have.

PREFACE

Over time, I came to love selling. It wasn't like that at first. When I first started out in sales, I was bad at it, I didn't like it, and it didn't work well for me. I wasn't that "natural born sales person." I don't believe in that anyway.

What led me to love selling, to eventually find success in sales, and to dedicate my career to it, were the lessons learned and the observations made while working to earn my commissions based on the value I gave to my clients. Along the way, I learned to execute my work with precision and discipline; and later in life, as I matured, to execute my work efficiently. For me, professional success was not worth much if it came at the expense of everything else that life had to offer.

The net result of all of this was a process-based approach to sales. It developed rather piecemeal at first. I would read books, listen to lectures, experiment with different techniques, and so forth. I kept what worked, threw out what didn't, and adapted these techniques to new selling situations over my twenty-plus year sales career.

When I started to work as a sales trainer and manager, I came to realize that executing with consistency in the context of a well-defined and developed sales process was in many ways as important as the execution of any specific technique. Both are important, but very few salespeople I worked with thought about the process. Most had various levels of skill around various techniques, but very few of them put together any kind of a coordinated effort at executing their work with discipline.

They would typically "do their thing" and sometimes sales would happen. Over time, the lucky, persistent, or talented ones got a few great accounts; some were more successful than others. The best revenue producers in the company often became the salespeople who were the best at "managing" their big accounts, but often that "account management" did not include any selling. In other words, they had grown some nice, big accounts that they were sustaining, but they were not actively pursuing new streams of business from inside or outside of their existing client base. Why is this a problem? Early in my sales career, I saw how tragic this approach could be.

I was working in San Francisco in the 1990s at a branch sales office of a national company. The office had about thirty salespeople. One of the top revenue producers, let's call him Bob, was making commissions in the neighborhood of $300,000 per year. Ninety percent of his income came from one company that had experienced enormous growth since Bob had started working with it.

Unfortunately, one day, a new purchasing manager was hired at Bob's client company, and this new purchasing manager did an audit. In the audit, it was discovered that Bob had been overcharging the client, and Bob was told to go away. Bob had forgotten how to generate new revenue streams, and was in the process of building a big new house; it was not so good to be Bob!

At that time, I was one of the new salespeople in the office. I was not making nearly as much money as the top producers, but I had worked out a lot of my selling systems, and was executing with fury. As a result, my numbers, as meager as they were in comparison with the "big hitters," were rising consistently. Bob, who would not even look at me in the hallway prior to his tragedy, all of a sudden tried to make friends with me, to see what I was doing to get new business on a consistent basis.

What he saw was that I had a selling system, and that I executed it with discipline. A far different approach from the passive account management approach that he had taken with his former, lucrative client.

Selling is about doing what it takes to get new business, from both new and existing clients, with a variety of prospecting techniques that vary from cold calls to, well, writing a book. Sales is not about telling jokes, meeting the right people at the right parties, or having the right connections (although those things can help). It is possible, and preferable, to sell in a systematic way. Those who do, tend to succeed consistently, even if they do get "Bobbed" from time to time.

It was observations like the Bob story, and many others, that led me to execute my own sales practice along a disciplined process, to train sales-people and sales managers around a process-based sales methodology, and to write this book. It is my hope that this book can help even more people get the knots out of their stomachs about how things will go this quarter, and just start executing with discipline, and winning the results that come with it—consistent sales growth and time to enjoy life.

David Masover
May 31, 2009
Budapest, Hungary

FOREWORD

Sales happen when the circumstances are right. But what are the right circumstances and what can we do to create them?

It is often said that sales is a numbers game—the more attempts we make, the more sales will result. Certainly, that is true. But wouldn't it be better to produce more sales without having to increase our level of effort? Of course, the answer is "yes". There is an entire industry dedicated to teaching us how to open a conversation, handle an objection, and countless other important tactics. The brute force application of tactics, however, is more costly in terms of time and lost opportunities than Masover's elegant application of correct strategy.

Over the course of my decades in business, I have seen a wide array of personalities succeed in sales. So the secret is not in morphing one's personality into a particular sales prototype. I have seen sales success across a range of products and services. So the secret is not entirely in the product being sold. I have superintended successful sales of products for pennies and services for hundreds of thousands of dollars. So success is not predestined by the price tag. But I have never seen a successful sale that did not conform to the pattern that Masover lays bare in this book.

Masover has reflected on his years of experience, his business endeavors, and his successes both big and small, to identify for you the invariant situations and practices that characterize every successful sale. By outlining the 7 events that create a successful sale, he provides a structured way to evaluate every sales opportunity and make better decisions about which to pursue and how. In addition, he supplies useful hints and anecdotes to help transform the mere prospect of a transaction into a successful sale.

I expect that sales will remain largely an art form for the rest of my life. But, as the saying goes, there is a method to this madness. Masover has exposed the pattern you seek as a salesperson. If you have been success-fully selling for years, his book will ring true and articulate what you have known but couldn't quite put into words. If you have been less successful than you'd like to be (and who isn't, really?), apply the lessons of this book. Either way, you will make more money and, maybe for the first time, you'll know why.

Jerry McLaughlin, CEO
Branders.com

WHO SHOULD READ THIS BOOK

This book is written for salespeople who would like to execute their job with more discipline, higher confidence, and greater effectiveness. The basic framework of the process described in the book is universal and, as such, can be applied to all forms of professional sales. My personal selling, managing, training, and consulting experience—and thus, the emphasis of this book—is in business-to-business selling in a small-to-medium-sized business environment.

This book is written for people who are new to sales, as well as for experienced salespeople and sales managers. It is my experience that plenty of experienced and even successful salespeople don't have any kind of consistent methodology with which they execute their job. (Read the preface for one such example). An experienced salesperson who reads this book and applies the methods to his or her current practices will find increased efficiency and effectiveness through the disciplined application of the things he or she may already be doing.

The book is written for the individual salesperson, but can easily be adapted to a group format. As such, there is a secondary potential audience for this book—anyone in sales management. Senior and front line sales managers can use this book as a guide for setting up a group-level structure for organized sales execution, management, and success. I have written an addendum to this book directed at sales managers and sales executives which illustrates how using the methodology described in this book can be applied to a group and used by management to manage, motivate and measure performance for their organization more effectively. Please visit www.davidmasover.com/manager-appendix to download this free addendum.

HOW TO USE THIS BOOK

This book is organized to illustrate the steps in the sales process and to allow readers to develop their own sales process and personal process-based sales activity plan.

Philosophy and Illustrative Concepts
Chapter 1 is somewhat philosophical in nature, and illustrates some concepts and supporting ideas that will be useful for readers to keep in mind as they go through the rest of the book.

Sales Steps, Shortcuts and Personalizing your Process
The rest of the book, Chapters 2 through 11, highlights specific steps in the sales process (Chapters 2, 3, 4, 6, 8, 9, and 10); a shortcut that may help get to a closed deal somewhere in the middle of the sales process (Chapters 5 and 7); and a way to finalize the development of the personal process-based sales activity plan (Chapter 11).

Location of Key Points and Exercises
At the end of each chapter, there is a list of key points and an exercise section. By completing the exercises at the end of each chapter and finalizing the plan by working it through the exercises in Chapter 11, readers will develop their personal process-based sales activity plan.

Following the chapters, there are Appendices to help develop some of the key sections of the plan.

21 Common Prospecting Methods
Appendix A describes the 21 common prospecting methods mentioned in Chapter 3 in greater detail, and illustrates ways to employ these prospecting methods into a personal process-based sales activity plan.

Phone Script Mini-Workshop
Appendix B is a mini-workshop in developing a script for a phone call to secure a meeting for the purposes of generating new business. This applies to the generation of new business from prospective customers, as well as from existing customers and referrals.

Prospecting Objection Handling Mini-Workshop
Appendix C covers ways to handle and overcome the specific objections that might arise when trying to set a meeting to discuss new business.

Sample Process-Based Sales Activity Plan
Appendix D is a sample process-based personal sales activity plan that allows readers to see a completed plan to serve as a guide in developing their own sales activity plan.

Manager and Executive Addendum
An addendum for sales managers and sales executives can be downloaded from www.davidmasover.com/manager-appendix at no charge. The addendum illustrates how managers and executives can apply the process-based systems described in the book in a group setting for both the benefit of the individual salesperson and for the management of the group as well.

Interactive, Resource-Rich Website
The website that accompanies the book, www.davidmasover.com, offers readers and community members a place to learn more about this book, contribute their own ideas, access additional resources, and network with other readers.

It is my greatest hope that all of this is as useful for you as the development of these practices has been for me in my own sales career, and for my colleagues, students, and clients during the ongoing course of my consulting practice.

TABLE OF CONTENTS

INTRODUCTION

Near the end of March of 2009, I made a financial commitment toward the publishing of this book, and I learned to ride a snowboard. Why on earth would I start my book this way? Because there is a relevant connection—Process!

Let me start with my tale of learning to snowboard. In December 2008, a friend persuaded me to drive a few hours to a local small ski area. At forty-three, I decided to try snowboarding for the first time. I was living in Hungary, and at the time, I did not speak the language well enough for any conversation more meaningful than ordering in a restaurant or finding my way when I was lost. The snowboard instructors at the Hungarian resort did not speak English, so I was on my own.

For the next few hours on that cold December day, I slid down the bunny hill, falling at least three times per run, on what was a very short run. At the end of each run, I struggled to make it up the rope tow without falling. I usually failed. In spite of this, for some warped reason that I can't explain, I liked snowboarding, in theory. In reality, I knew that whatever I was doing that day, could not honestly be called snowboarding.

On the way home, my friend told me that he wanted to go again the following week. I agreed, and decided that I could harness the power of the Internet to help me do better next time. So I went home, logged on, and proceeded to read articles and study snowboarding lessons on YouTube. That next week, I started my second day of snowboarding full of hope and optimism. I had seen how learning was supposed to progress, and I was determined to follow the path that I had been shown.

That second time, I did a little bit better, but not much. That was good news for the makers of Advil, but not for my old, tired knees and back, which really, really hurt.

My friend is very persuasive. A few months later, he convinced my whole family to come with his family on a weeklong ski vacation to Austria. This time, I was determined to succeed. Luckily, there was more than just my determination going for me this time. Determination alone had not been enough to yield success in my first two efforts.

At our ski resort in Austria, many of the instructors spoke English, and I was able to sign up for a group lesson for beginners. Interestingly enough, the teaching system that the instructor used was very similar to what I had seen on YouTube. The difference was that I was able to get instruction and feedback in real time as I practiced the incremental steps they were teaching me.

To make a long story short, it took only two days of instruction to become good enough to practice on my own. By the sixth and last day of our vacation, I slid down a long ski run on the mountain (on my snowboard) with my five-year-old son who had just learned to ski. I was not yet doing any fancy tricks or any of those flippy things you see on the soda commercials, but I was good enough by that time to keep my eyes on my son, stay with him, and feel confident that I could both get down the slope and provide some parental support while exercising my new snowboarding skills.

By following a systematic learning process, practicing what I learned with discipline, and getting expert help along the way, I was able to achieve a level of competence that allowed me to function, and even to enjoy my newly acquired skills in a meaningful way.

Following a well-developed process, practicing with discipline, and getting help along the way seems to work best in a sales environment as well.

This book is about the sales process, the way it should be, but not for the sake of process, rather for the sake of providing support and assistance to salespeople in their efforts to make sales. By following the practices and principles outlined in this book, I, along with many of my colleagues, students, and clients have learned to execute sales efforts with meaningful levels of success, and often in less time and with less effort than before.

CHAPTER 1

Preliminary Considerations for Successful Process Selling

Before getting into the process itself, this first chapter will focus on some groundwork—a solid foundation for the process. I start with a definition of sales, to make sure that we are all talking about the same thing.

(NOTE: There is some important information in this chapter. Information that will help you to be more successful with your sales process by making sure that you are properly oriented mentally and that you have the right attitudes about your job and your potential for contribution to your clients. However, if you need to get started right away on the sales process itself, then skip ahead to the next chapter.)

Definitions

There is an old legend that Vince Lombardi, the famously successful coach of the Green Bay Packers (US professional football team), started each new season the same way. He would stand up in front of his team, a group of top performing, highly seasoned veterans of the game, hold a football in the air, and declare, *"Gentlemen, this is a football."*

I don't have any kind of a ball, but I would also like to clear up any misconceptions about what we are talking about here before I start. This seems necessary since the word "sales" has several perceived meanings, many of which are negative. What kind of negativity?

Take for example, the classic sales joke:

> *Question: How can you tell when a salesperson is lying?*
> *Answer: His lips are moving.*

Or the old definition of a salesperson as someone who is *too lazy to work but too honest to steal*.

Or the fact that there is so much stigma around the word "sales," that no shortage of alternative job titles have been created to describe the work, such as:

- Account Manager
- Customer Relationship Specialist
- Business Development Manager
- Etc.

I, for one, am quite proud to be involved in the profession of sales, and much of that pride is based on how I think about sales and how I define it. Allow me to clear up what I mean by sales right from the start, primarily to make sure that the message of this book is properly oriented. As a bonus, maybe more of us can start feeling even better about our work as sales professionals.

As a point of departure, it must be acknowledged that every real, honest company that exists needs revenue. This even applies to non-profit organizations, charitable organizations, and religious institutions of all kinds. If we can agree on that, then we should also be able to agree that there is usually someone in each organization who is responsible for making contact with people or companies that might transfer some of their money to that organization in exchange for something (product, service, the warm fuzzy feeling that comes from helping others, etc.).

The person who makes contact with the potential sources of revenue and tries to persuade them to direct their money toward his or her organization is the person I am talking about when I say "salesperson." Regardless of job title or other job responsibilities, for the sake of our definition, this person operates as a "salesperson" with at least some of their time.

The Right Mindset

Now that we can agree on what a salesperson is responsible for, let's talk about the right way for a salesperson to think about the job of selling. Why is this important? To illustrate, let's go back to the snowboarding story from the Introduction:

In the group lesson that I had in Austria, nine people signed up. Four of the students seemed to pick up the instructions easily, and were among the first to jump up and try something new when the teacher asked us to do so.

Three of the students were a bit more reluctant to try, but did so with only a few grunts and groans; they also picked up the skills as they were taught.

Two of the students were unable to keep up with the class, took a lot of extra time from the teacher, and were eventually moved into their own group so that the rest of the class could progress more quickly.

Over the four days of my trip that followed the group lessons, I saw many of my classmates on the "blue" rated (easy) runs on which we all practiced. The seven of us who were able to pick up instructions during the class, generally speaking, were practicing our turns and working to gain control. We were snowboarding.

The two students, who struggled in class, were still using techniques from the first day of the class—sliding down the hill on the edge of their board, analogous to snow plowing for skiers, or riding with training wheels for bike riders.

What I noticed about these two, while we were in class, was fear. They were afraid of falling. They were not confident in their abilities. They seemed to be more worried about what the other people in class thought about them than about finding a way to succeed.

In other words, their attitude about snowboarding was limiting their ability to learn and execute the skills required to succeed.

I see this in salespeople far too often—fear of engagement, lack of confidence, more concern with how others think of them than with getting results. In my experience, this problem can be easy to fix, but in spite of that, it is quite prevalent. Let's address it here before getting into the process itself. If our collective heads are in the right place before we start, we'll be much more effective in learning what we need to learn to succeed.

A strong self-perception can certainly be influenced by the way that a salesperson thinks about the job of selling. Towards that end, the above definition of a salesperson should be an important source of pride for salespeople. Since companies can't survive without revenue, and revenue generation is a sales function, the value of the sales role is clear, but the definition alone does not explain my aforementioned pride.

The correct self-perception, or mindset if you will, can and should be an even greater source of pride. Beyond that, this mindset is strong enough, if sincerely believed and practiced, to overcome the fear and reluctance felt by many otherwise ambivalent and ineffective salespeople. What is that mindset that salespeople should adopt in order to feel great about their work? It is this:

I am an expert in my field. My job is to help qualified prospects make good decisions about solving problems using my product or service.

If you can come to believe that this is true about your job, then it is easy to feel good about it—don't you think?

So how can we convince ourselves that this is true? Most easily, if it is true—so let's look at what we need to do, piece-by-piece, to make this real.

I am an expert in my field.

Imagine that you go to a camera store to buy a digital camera, and you ask the person behind the counter a question about megapixels, battery life, or some other feature of the camera you might like to buy. Compare these two scenarios: In case number one, the salesperson grabs the box and starts scanning the box for an answer. In case number two, he answers your question by giving you information showing that he understands your concerns and is knowledgeable about the different cameras you are considering. Which one makes you feel like this person can help you make your purchase decision?

To best serve both your customers and yourself as a sales professional, you should strive to learn as much as you can about everything related to your business; the business of your clients and how they use your product; why competitive products might be better, worse, or different from yours; and so on. Leave no stone unturned, and make the learning process ongoing. This is one of the most important ways that you can provide value to your client.

Whether you know it and whether you like it or not, your customers expect you to have the answers to questions that relate to how they will use your products and how your products compare to their other choices (your competition, other solutions to their current situation, etc.). If you don't have this information, you are severely disadvantaged. If you get a question that your client knows is obscure, you can get away with a sincere,*"That's a great question. Let me do some research on that and get right back to you with an answer."* Assuming that you do get back to them, you might be OK here, but this will only work a few times before they see you as a resource no better than Google, or the information printed on the box. It is hard to have pride in your job in this event—mostly because you don't deserve it. It's also hard to do your job well—the part of the job that includes closing the deal will be harder if the client doesn't see you as an expert in the field of your own products or services.

My job is to help qualified prospects...
Did you ever get one of those birthday candles that you couldn't blow out? Frustrating at first, they end up funny. There is nothing funny about trying to sell to someone who does not have the ability or the proclivity to buy from you—just frustration. If you don't qualify well, you will waste a lot of time trying to sell to people who are unable and/or unwilling to say "yes" to you about your offer (more on this in the chapter on qualification). It will be hard for you to feel good about your job if you keep going through the motions of the sales process but rarely get anywhere. Qualify well and the rest will be easier, and much more fulfilling as well.

...*make a good decision...*

As implied above, your prospective customers want information from you, but for a specific reason. If your prospective customers are talking to you, they either are inclined to waste time, or they have a decision to make and they are talking to you because they think that you might be able to help them with it. Determine that the latter is the case (again, qualification), and you will get tremendous satisfaction if you successfully assist your prospect in making the best purchase decision.

...*about solving a problem...*

The satisfaction only increases when you realize that the decision they are trying to make solves a real problem for them. With your help, if you do your job right, they will be better off for having spoken to you because you helped them both to make a decision they can feel good about, and to solve the problem that got you into the conversation with them in the first place.

...*using my product or service.*

OK, let's not kid ourselves here. The job is called "sales," and the goal is to get the prospect to buy YOUR product or service. In this context, a professional salesperson should NEVER sell something he or she does not believe in. The whole thing falls apart as soon as you try to sell ice cubes to Eskimos, holes to bagels ... you get the idea.

Alternatively, a salesperson who:

- is an expert
- knows the product and the competition
- knows how to solve the problems that typical customers may face
- believes in the product or service offered

is a good choice, and indeed and asset to the customer. This salesperson is not only valuable to the customer, but is also in a position to feel quite good about the work and the value that is provided to the customer. "I'm here to help" is a much nicer thing to believe about your work than "I'm here to sell you something." The latter is always true if you are in sales. If the former is not only true, but also predominant in the mind of the salesperson, then the job is not only easier, it is more fulfilling as well.

Remember, you are the expert, your job is to help, and when you do that with pride and integrity, you will feel better about your job, and your client will feel better about the job you do as well.

The Value of a Process-Based Orientation

So now that we know what sales is, and how we should think about ourselves as sales professionals, the next logical preliminary question is this: What does it mean to operate with a process-based orientation? Let's start answering that question with a definition:

Merriam-Webster's Online Dictionary defines "process" as...

a series of actions or operations conducing to an end.

When most salespeople get into a selling situation, they are looking for clues about what the client is thinking to help them understand where they stand with respect to the possibility of making a sale.

Even if the salesperson asks all of the right qualifying, closing, or open-ended questions, the answers that are given by the client often happen without the benefit of a road map. Without a process against which these questions and the progress of the sales discussion can be measured and evaluated, it is easy to get lost.

This is how a sales process can anchor and orient your efforts. As the definition states, it is a *series of actions* designed to *reach a specific result.*

With a well-defined and well-executed sales process, the information that a salesperson receives from the client is constantly measured against a map—where am I now, where do I need to go, and what do I need to do in order to get the conversation to move there. It helps to answer the most fundamental, and often forgotten sales question: *"What's next?"*

There is an old joke about a husband and wife on a driving trip. The wife looks at the map and proclaims that they are lost. The husband agrees, but adds that in spite of that, they are making great time.

You won't know how well you are doing without a benchmark to measure against, and revenue goals at the end of the process won't tell you how to get there. You need a map to follow along the way. The sales process is that map. If sales is a journey, then the map, the process, is imminently valuable.

What is the Universal Sales Process?

The sales process model that we will use in this book is simple. This does not mean that it is not complete, important, or useful; it is just simple. I postulate that EVERY sales process follows this model. Many other names exist for these stages, but these are the steps that should be done and, in fact, need to be done for each and every kind of sale to be completed:

Leads: Some subset of the six billion plus people who live on our planet should be the target of your prospecting efforts. These people are your leads. This includes your existing customers when viewed as potential sources of new business.

Prospecting: Prospecting is the act of engaging and then convincing a lead to enter into a dialogue with you about making a sale.

Qualification: Once you are in that dialogue, you should first make sure the person is capable of and likely to buy from you. This is qualification.

Needs Analysis: Once it looks like the prospective client is capable of and likely to buy from you, you need to find out what exactly they need, and what they might want or need enough to exchange for some of their money.

Presenting the Solution: Once you understand their needs, you should suggest a way that those needs can be met by some product or service that you or the organization you represent can provide. You also need to let them know the cost of those products or services.

Objections / Negotiations: Once you suggest a solution and a price, you may face some questions or objections, and you may need to negotiate some of the items in the proposal.

Close: If all of that gets done, you will want to secure an agreement to complete the order, contract, proposal, and so forth. This is called "closing the deal," or more simply, the close.

In selling the services of my own sales consulting practice, and in providing these consulting services to my clients, this seven-step sales process is always the starting point. This process applies to every kind of sale imaginable, from retail sales in a store to the sale of professional services and everything in between. To see this illustrated, please visit this book's website at www.davidmasover.com and click on "process models" in the "download forms" section to see the sales process of a variety of professions modeled in step-by-step detail.

By working through each of these seven steps for each client, each sales situation, and each prospective negotiation, a map of how to move forward and through the process, how to measure success, and how to improve the likelihood for success will become clear. In the chapters that follow, each step will be reviewed in more detail, and later, we'll see what we can do with the process as a whole.

NOTE: If you have a sales process that differs substantially from the one I have just described, please visit the website for this book at www.davidmasover.com and click on the "contact us" button to tell me about it. If it is indeed something new or different, I will add it to my website and include it in the next edition of this book, credited to you.

With Respect to the Sales Process, "What's New?" Is Not the Right Question

When you are simply trying to sell something, an answer to the question *"what's new?"* is a good thing to have. It can buy you at least a few moments of time from an interested prospect. What you do with it from there is up to you.

With respect to the entire sales process, however, I have come to believe that this is a useless question. People ask it, because they don't know what else to ask. Much like a prospective client who will ask about price if you don't show him some value, a person interested in sales process improvement will ask *"what's new"* for lack of a better question.

There are some new things that you can do within the sales process, and there will be some new ideas in this book, but the sales process itself is not new, and it doesn't need to be in order to be effective.

What is important, is that the process is properly customized to your specific sales situation, and that you execute the process well. Reading this book, and following the exercises will help you do both.

If you want to be successful in sales, any time, any place, and in any industry or product sector, you need to do the following:

1. Find someone to talk to (Prospecting)
2. Determine that they are capable of buying your product (Qualification)
3. Figure out what exactly they want or need enough to spend money on (Needs Analysis)
4. Suggest something for them to buy (Proposal)
5. Address any questions, concerns or bargaining attempts (Objections and Negotiations)
6. Close the deal (Closing)

These six elements, plus finding some source of leads to feed into the prospecting stage, are the sales process for every sale, always, and in every industry sector. Nothing is new here. However, operating effectively within the context of this foundational level of sales is critical to efficient and ongo-ing success. These are the principles, the philosophy, and the framework for operating tactics upon which all successful sales efforts will stand.

When I speak internationally about the sales process, I am asked a lot about how it works in different cultures, industries, and with varying sell cycles. The fact is, this part of the sales game is the same everywhere, as well as in every time. Don't get me wrong, culture is important, as is industry and other specific considerations. That is why we will need to work at person-alizing the sales process for each specific situation, even for each specific salesperson. But be clear. Failure to execute within a well-defined process will severely limit your effectiveness and efficiency. If you get the cultural stuff and the industry stuff right, but fail to work within a well-defined process, your culturally appropriate behaviors will be much less efficient and effective than if you apply them within the context of a well-defined process. The rest of this book will support that statement, so read on.

What I intend to show you is that the sales process holds the key to a fundamental improvement in front line sales execution, efficiency, and effectiveness. We'll spend the rest of the book talking about that. But be forewarned. Very few things are new here—just what works.

The comments I so often get on the feedback forms of my sales trainings on sales process sum up this point nicely. In almost every such training, I get a few comments that are some variation of the following:

"I didn't learn anything new, but I finally understand how it all is supposed to work together, and what I am supposed to do in order to be successful."

That is what sales process can do for you, and that is the focus of this book.

Front Loading

In our definition of salespeople, I mentioned the common perception that we salespeople, as a group, are too lazy to work and too honest to steal. I don't want to reinforce the first part of that statement, but it is going to sound like it here!

My sales process has seven steps. However, as you read through the steps, you will see that there is no need to get through all seven steps in order to finish the process.

For example, if you address the objections during needs analysis, there is no need to bother with them later. If you determine the budget in the qualification stage, there is no need to argue about it later. Chapter 6 provides a tactic for closing after step 2, qualification. Chapter 8 provides an elegant closing technique to be used after needs analysis. If you follow the process and cover all of the required items, then it is possible to close early. These are all examples of the kind of front loading that will be discussed throughout the book, and throughout the process.

This relates to the old joke about the salesperson who was in the middle of a well-prepared presentation when the client jumped up and said, *"OK, I'll buy it!"* to which the salesperson replied, *"Now just wait; I'm not done with my presentation."*

The concept of "Front Loading" is a key part of the process. While the whole process is designed to lead to an easy and effective close, it is also designed to allow closing opportunities along the way. Make note of this: if you execute well, your seven-step process could be quite a bit shorter. If not shorter, then you will get the hard parts out of the way early, and you will ensure early on that the rest of the process is worth pursuing, and likely to be successful. Now is that laziness, or are we just saving everyone a bunch of time?

What's Missing

So by now, we know what we mean by "salespeople," we know what the right mindset is, we know why process is important, and we know that we want to create shortcuts in the process by front loading wherever possible.

Will effective execution of the right sales process complete the picture? Mostly, but there are a few important things we won't cover too much in this book, so let me mention them here.

Skills

We are going to "glide" over the subject of raw sales skills here. Skills are specific ways of doing things that work in a sales context, like establishing rapport, probing with open-ended questions, and getting the client to agree to make a decision at the end of some set of communications before the communication even starts. Sales skills are critical to success, and the quest for sales skills should be an ongoing part of every salesperson's development ... so why leave them out of this book?

First of all, there is no shortage of other places where a salesperson can learn skills. Therefore, we will focus on the part of the overall package that is not as thoroughly addressed elsewhere. More importantly, while skills are important, they are much more effective when they are executed within the context of a well-defined process. We'll spend the rest of the book talking about exactly what that means and how to do it. This book will help you build the processes that become the context within which you can execute, test, and measure your skills, a foundation from which the likelihood and efficiency of sales success is greatly improved.

Furthermore, by tracking the execution of sales skills through a process, it is easy to see which skills, or which areas of the process, need work. Skills out of this context are just not as potent or visible as skills in this context. For those reasons, we will focus here on the context more than on the skills themselves.

Tracking systems

There is an old saying: "If it isn't being measured, then it isn't being managed." For the purposes of this book, tracking is important—in fact, critical—but a specific tracking system is not the focus here. For our purposes, any CRM including an excel spread sheet is OK. The element we will consider here is the importance of tracking the big pieces of the process, and the recognition of what needs to happen in the current step before you move onto the next step in the process. Any decent CRM system can help with that. It is the definitions, agreements, and execution of the elements in the process that will make the ultimate difference, not the specific tracking system. Don't get me wrong; tracking is vitally important, but for our purposes, the specific tracking system is not.

Review of Key Points

Chapter 1
Preliminary Considerations for Successful Process Selling

- If considered the right way, the profession of sales, properly conducted, is certainly something in which the salesperson can be proud.
- Selling and the sales process are not new, but like many crafts, the secret to success lies not in the novelty, but in the disciplined execution along a proven and well-considered path.
- Thinking about selling the right way—that you are an expert who can help a prospective client make a good buying decision—goes a long way to instilling pride and effectiveness in sales efforts, and usually results in happy clients as well.
- Executing sales along a proven, polished, and disciplined process is more efficient and effective than random effort—no matter how strong that effort may be.
- While a process is a good thing, there is no rule that says you need to get all of the way through the process to be done. Front loading will help you move through the process with lots of closing opportunities along the way.
- All professional selling follows the same seven step process:
    1. Generating leads
    2. Prospecting
    3. Qualification
    4. Needs Analysis
    5. Solution
    6. Objections and Negotiations
    7. Closing the deal
- Analyzing your own sales process is the right way to begin developing your own process-based, results-focused, front-loaded sales action plan.

Exercises

- Consider the way you go about making sales today. Map your own sales activity along the seven-point sales process described in this chapter. Do you cover all of the steps? Are you systematic about how you work through it?

  - The benefit of doing this now, before you read the book and rebuild your sales process, is that it will serve as the "before" part of the "before and after" comparison. Be honest, and by the end of the book, look back on this exercise so that you can see what changes you have made based on the work you do as you read through the book and complete the exercises.

CHAPTER 2

Sales Process Step #1: Leads

Definition of Leads

Leads are all of the prospective customers in your target area who you think might do business with you, and who you are able to contact. For example, if you sold dental supplies in a local area, then the listings for dentists, orthodontists, etc., in the phone book for that local area would be your leads. They meet the definition of your prospective clients (people using dental supplies in your local area), and you can contact them (the phone book listing almost always has a phone number).

Some Thoughts About the Leads Step in the Process

There is not a lot to say about leads, but two important things can make you much more efficient and effective if you adhere to them:

1. You need some good sources of leads that will supply you on an ongoing basis.

I spent a good portion of the "formative years" of my career in the promotional products industry. Promotional products are all of those usable items like coffee mugs, pens, and T-shirts that companies put their logos on for marketing purposes. I struggled for a long time, trying to find just the right market to target, and a big barrier was the lack of a consistent source of "hot" leads.

Trade show exhibitors are a major target market for promotional items. In order to reach them, I first started trying to identify them by attending local trade shows to get the published, hard copy of the directory of exhibitors. Then I would call exhibitors from that show who were in my local area with the idea that if they exhibited at the local show, they probably exhibited at more shows as well. I had mixed results. Getting to the shows cost me a lot of time, and by the time I had the book, that show was over for the prospects, so the urgency of their next purchase was not always so high.

As the Internet evolved, I found my optimal solution. Websites began to appear that listed trade shows by category, date, and location. Links to the trade show sites, which often included exhibitor lists, were usually included. My process then became quite easy. I simply backed out the typical production time of the promotional products, added some time for a decision-making process, and added an extra month. This added up to about three months. Then all I had to do was visit the websites that listed the trade shows and the trade show exhibitors, search for trade shows coming up three months ahead, and call the exhibitors in my local area. Each exhibitor I called had a potential upcoming opportunity with a firm date when delivery was required. I did not sell to all of them, but my hit rate got much better, my efficiency was much higher, and my career took off.

Each industry is different. Some have more obvious sources of leads than others. The important thing is that you work to find sources of leads that are more like a flowing hose than a glass of water. Spending your time looking for leads is much less productive than spending your time contacting leads and trying to turn them into prospects, so find an ongoing source of leads, and allow yourself to remain focused on the more productive parts of the sales process.

Don't forget that your existing clients are also a source of leads. Just don't let them be your only source of leads.

2. You should have a list of leads with contact information ready before you start your prospecting efforts. Then you should focus your efforts on getting through that list before you move on to other things.

This practice is sometimes referred to as "batching" with respect to time management. When you batch similar activities together, you experience greater efficiency due to the lower level of "switching costs," or the time it takes to transition from one kind of activity to another.

This section could just as well be a part of the prospecting section of the book, but since we are talking about leads, let's also focus on how to maximize the potential for return on each lead. In this context, we will discuss this idea now.

It amazes me that most salespeople I work with manage their leads in a very haphazard way. If a lead comes their way, they sit on it for a while, then find a time to call, usually tucked into the middle of other unrelated tasks. Perhaps they never heard of batching!

When I first started selling, I was terrible at cold calling. I finally found a good approach by reading and adopting ideas learned from the sales classic, *Cold Calling Techniques: That Really Work* by Stephan Schiffman.

One of the pieces of advice that he suggested in the book was really help-ful: Don't plan to make calls to your leads all day, rather, perhaps for just an hour.* However, in that hour, focus your efforts on NOTHING other than those calls. Have a list of names and phone numbers ready, eliminate all distractions, and do NOTHING but dial the phone for the thirty, sixty, or ninety minutes that you dedicate to your calls. In this way, you will manage the leads you worked hard to get in the most efficient and effective manner.

NOTE: Prospecting calls are not always cold calls, but prospecting calls are an integral part of your business. In this book, we will refer to them as Sales COmmunication REquests (SCORE). I will explain this concept in more detail in the sections on prospecting and in Appendix B, but for now, do not worry that this is a book on cold calling. It is not.

Contacting leads can be a psychologically stressful activity. To improve your chances of success, focus. Without focus, many salespeople give up after a few attempts, usually in the form of doing some other activity like im-mediately fulfilling the request of the last contact, then getting distracted by anything else that may come by. Remember, the calls are not fun, so any distraction looks better than making the next call.

Setting a specific time or number of dials goal and having the list of leads ready to go before you start is a great way to ensure that you will complete your goal. Not having this information ready before you start will ensure inefficiency (you shouldn't be looking up a new phone number between each call) and likely lead to distraction.

The combination of psychological stress and infinite distractions can derail your efforts completely. Several recent workplace productivity studies suggest that as much as fifteen minutes can be lost when a task that requires mental focus is interrupted. In other words, it can take up to fifteen minutes to regain focus on a serious piece of work when that work-related focus is interrupted. So checking email, getting up for a coffee, looking up your next phone number, researching the next company you call on the Internet, or taking an incoming call can be very expensive.

Furthermore, without a specific, predetermined amount of time or number of calls to make as a goal, most salespeople give up after a small number of attempts. They may dial the phone five times, get bad results, and decide it is not worth the effort. This conclusion is based on an insufficient sample size, and will most likely not lead to any significant results. Consider some of my own experiences.

When I first learned to cold call, I dedicated one-hour-a-day, three-days-a-week to cold calling. That doesn't sound like much, but I literally did nothing else during those sixty minutes; and after those sixty minutes, I was tired!

Before I started, I made sure that I had all of my phone numbers and names in front of me, my tally sheet*, my phone, and a note pad for any notes I might have to take—that was it. My phone was forwarded to voice mail, my pager (remember those?) was turned off and my email was easy to ignore, as it was not yet in widespread use. The focus was pure— 100 percent focus on cold calling as many times as possible in the prescribed time frame.

*You can find and download a sample of a simple tally sheet by visiting www. davidmasover.com. Go to the "download forms" section, and click on "lead tally sheet."

Over time, I began to see a pretty consistent pattern. In each hour, I could dial the phone about 33 times. I would talk to about five or six prospects in that hour, and set, on average, 1.5 meetings. That means that 27 or 28 times in that hour I dialed the phone with no contact at all, and at least 75 percent of the time I reached someone, I got a negative reaction. It would have been easy to give up if I had focused on the negative aspect of those results.

However, I neither gave up nor focused solely on the negative.

A more useful perspective was that every 40 minutes of activity led me to a meeting. Since I typically made a sale in 50 percent of my meetings and 50 percent of new customers who bought from me once turned into repeat clients, then the math worked out to one repeat client per every 160 minutes of calling. Extrapolating further, this meant that approximately one hour of cold calling three-days-a-week would have resulted in about 50 repeat clients per year. That was more than I could handle. However, it would have never been possible if I had given up or gotten distracted after a few calls.

So as you can imagine, after about six months, I had a time management problem: too many new clients to allow time for more cold calling. I solved this problem (see the sections in Chapter 11 on Database Maintenance and Bringing It All Together for more on this), but it was a positive problem to create and to then solve. For me, this was the precursor of the process method. Do what you do with precision and focus and you will get great results without huge investments of time. The time you save can be used to smash your way into sales superstardom, or to balance a high-income career with a life outside of work—all good goals, all achievable with focus.

False Sense of Urgency

When I suggest a focused block of time to contact leads, many sales-people immediately reject the idea of turning off their voice mail or email for even a short time during the day. They believe that they should always be available to their clients, no matter what. For this reason, they cannot commit to even thirty minutes per week of focused, proactive work.

If this is your opinion as well, then please forgive my blunt reply, but this is patently wrong! Every day, salespeople leave their email to go to lunch, go to a meeting, or go to the bathroom and wind up talking about the big game or the cool TV show for fifteen minutes on their way back. Mobile phones get turned off or ignored during presentations, client meetings, meetings with the boss, etc. None of your clients expect you to be available at their beck and call, and if they do, you have allowed them to have inappropriate expectations of you. This kind of a client relationship is neither healthy nor necessary.

Do yourself a favor. Try an experiment. Turn off all incoming communications for thirty minutes a day for one week and see how many things really explode. Your ego may be a bit bruised to find that the world does not stop when you are not fully reachable at every moment of the day, but your career will improve dramatically if you use those thirty minutes to get the sales process started for some new opportunities.

The Best Source of Leads

Without a doubt, the best source of leads are your existing clients. Be sure to think of them as leads for new business. Don't fall into the trap of complacency that turns you into an account managing order taker. Even your existing clients—*especially* your existing clients—need to be and deserve to be qualified for each new sale, given the courtesy of a needs analysis (that well may uncover more needs than your originally presumed), etc. We list existing clients as a source of leads in the chapter and in the appendix on prospecting. I'm not concerned that you will forget them, but you may forget to treat them as sources of NEW business, which is where your complacency comes in. Don't let this happen to you, or I may need to use your name instead of Bob in the preface of the second edition!

You Are Ready to Move on From This Step When

You are done with the step of leads when you have a specific target for a request for a conversation, and a way to reach them. This target can be a name and a phone number, name and a company, or even a company and a specific job function (so that you can ask the receptionist to connect you). Different situations and different salespeople will dictate different interpretations. Some believe that you must have a name and direct dial number, others, just a company. The specifics are not as important as the fact that you are ready to make an effort to engage without any further research or filtering. You may need to get past a gatekeeper or two, but if you are ready to make an effort to communicate, then you have a lead, and are ready to prospect.

Review of Key Points

Chapter 2
Sales Process Step #1: Leads

- Leads are simply everyone in your target geographic area who you think might do business with you, and people who you are able to contact.
- The best lead sources will provide leads on an ongoing basis rather than as a one-time event.
- Lead generation, like all phases of the process, should be done as a distinct activity, and should have a dedicated amount of time, energy, money, and/or effort allocated to it. Catching a lead by chance is great, but back that up with a systematic approach.
- Compile your leads in such a way that you can execute the next step, prospecting, without slowing down to sort through your leads.
- Don't allow yourself to be managed by the tasks of your day at the expense of the front end of your sales process. If you do, your sales results WILL suffer.

Exercises

- Identify sources of leads that can provide you with an ongoing flow of new leads that are appropriate for your business. Keep in mind that the prospecting method you choose may influence the lead sources that are best for you, and vice versa. Be sure to include criteria for your leads (location, revenue, number of employees, or whatever is appropriate for your own targets).
- Create some kind of a simple form or system on which to list your lead contact information once you get it. This will allow you to make your contacts with focus and disciplined execution, rather than requiring that you scramble to find a new phone number after each conversation.
- As a part of your lead management process, choose a specific amount of time and schedule prospecting time each week. The amount will depend on many factors, but try to set aside a few time periods each

week of at least thirty minutes each when you can focus on contacting your leads. In my experience, the first half of the morning is the best time to reach people. Later in the day, most people have had their own plan for the day derailed by unexpected surprises. Be an unexpected surprise that comes earlier in the day, and you may be more welcome than later on.

CHAPTER 3
Sales Process Step #2: Prospecting

Definition of Prospecting

Prospecting is the act of making an attempt to request a forum for sales-related communication from someone who you believe could be a qualified prospect.

Some Thoughts About the Prospecting Step in the Process

Prospecting is one of the main areas where salespeople fail. They don't do enough of it, and when they do it, they don't do so in a focused, targeted, specific, or effective manner. The reasons for this include a lack of imagination about how to prospect, and a lack of strategy about how to execute the prospecting effort to best support success in later stages of the sales process. Let's see what we can do to fix that.

When I talk to salespeople about prospecting, they immediately think of cold calling to people they don't know. While cold calling is indeed a form of prospecting, it is one of at least 21 prospecting methods that I use as a starting point when discussing methods of prospecting with my clients. Here is my list of 21, which is always open to further additions—no upwards limit here. If you can think of a way to prospect that is not on this list, please visit the website of this book at www.davidmasover.com and click on the "contact us" button to tell me about it. If it is indeed something new or different, I will add it to my website, and include it in the next edition of this book, credited to you.

Proactive Prospecting Methods
1. Cold Calling
2. Company-generated Leads
3. Networking
4. Trade Associations
5. Formal Networking Groups
6. Referrals and Introductions
7. Electronic Networking Groups
8. Existing Customers
9. Former Customers

Message-Based Prospecting Methods
10. Seminars (presenting)
11. Conferences (presenting)
12. Trade Shows (exhibiting)
13. Articles (or books)
14. Newsletters
15. Getting quoted in the media
16. Blogs (including community-based forums)

Passive Prospecting Methods
17. Advertisements
18. Community Activity
19. Sponsorship
20. Special Events
21. Direct Mail (or email)

Each of these methods will be addressed in detail in Appendix A, but for now, let's look at them from a more general perspective:

Generally speaking, and in spite of this long list, there are really only two kinds of prospecting methods listed here:

1. Contacting someone who has never heard of you to request a forum for sales communication (also known as cold calling—a favorite of salespeople everywhere). This is the first item on the list. Technically, it can be done in person, by phone, or by email.

2. Doing something that sets up an opportunity to contact someone to request a forum for sales communication. This is represented by everything else on the list, and anything else you can think of as a prospecting method that is not on this list. This can be referred to as "warming up" a cold call.

The goal of prospecting is to set up an opportunity to communicate with a prospect so that you can qualify them, sell to them, and close them. Everything at the front end of the sales process should be directed at this goal. Sounds obvious, right? Before you answer, think about how most salespeople and companies approach some of these prospecting efforts.

Are you a member of LinkedIn, Xing, or some other online networking group? If so, how do you use it to generate business opportunities? Most people set up a profile, wait for something to happen, and soon start to wonder why they even bother to be there. See Appendix A for a more pro-active approach here.

Have you ever exhibited at a trade show and came back with nothing substantial to work with? Perhaps with some lead cards or business cards, but did you really maximize that opportunity? Did you even follow up with the leads from the show to try to set up a meeting? Many people don't even do this—what a wasted effort!

Have you ever presented at a seminar? Was the presentation designed to set up the sales conversation? Did you do what most people do who present at a seminar—try to sound smart and hope that people will recognize that and call you after the seminar for some more of the wisdom you have? They probably won't.

The common thread here is that the strategic planning for these three examples, and even many cold calls, does not start with the simple, focused idea that the goal of prospecting is to get the opportunity for sales communication. If you are not having a sales communication with someone, you are not selling, and you are not engaged in the process. Accordingly, EVERY properly executed prospecting effort should be directed at one thing, and one thing only—giving you a REASON to ask for a sales communication with a prospective customer.

Appendix B is designed to be a mini-workshop to help you develop the "Sales Communication Request" call (SCORE). I'll give away a bit of the secret here, but don't let this stop you from doing the Appendix B exercise to develop your full approach.

The secret to a successful SCORE is having the right "reason." Anytime you get on the phone or into a conversation with someone to set up a SCORE, you should be able to tell them:

The reason I am calling you is _____.

That reason should be relevant for the person you are speaking with, and should lead to an opportunity for the sales communication. See Appendix B for a more detailed discussion.

Let's see how this plays out using our three examples above:

LinkedIn (email):
Dear _____, I am sending you this message because (*the reason always comes as a "because"*) your profile here on LinkedIn is similar to that of many of my current clients. I provide companies like yours with (*insert your service here*) and I wanted to know if you would like to learn more about it. If so, please contact me and I would be happy to (*call, email, meet, send*) you more information about our service offering.

Trade show follow up (telephone):
Hi _____, this is (*me*) from (*my company*). The reason I am calling is to follow up on our meeting at the (*trade show name here*). I would like to learn more about the details of your situation and to suggest some solutions that have worked well for some of our clients. Are you available for a meeting next Tuesday at 10:00?

Seminar follow up (telephone):

Hi _____, this is (*me*) from (*my company*). The reason I am calling is to follow up on the seminar last week. Since we were only able to talk about (*the subject of the seminar*) in general terms at the seminar, I wanted to follow up with you now to see if it makes sense to meet in person so that we can discuss your situation in detail, and to see if the things that we discussed at the seminar might be worth considering for implementation inside of your company. Are you available for a meeting next Tuesday at 10:00?

In each of these examples, the prospecting method is used in the follow up call (the SCORE) as the REASON for the call, and the springboard from which to request the meeting. Your prospecting methods will be much more successful if you keep this in mind as you decide how to design your prospecting methods, how to execute them, and what exactly you do as a part of your prospecting efforts to set up the reason for the call in the SCORE.

What I just shared with you is extremely simple, extremely powerful, and usually missed. Let me repeat here. Every prospecting effort should be designed to create a REASON to contact a prospect and to request a meeting or a phone call—some kind of sales communication. If your prospecting methods are designed this way, you will be very efficient and effective in your efforts to set meetings. The goal is to get a meeting or some other form of conversation about selling your product to the other person. Design and execute the prospecting effort with that goal squarely in mind to improve your chances of reaching it.

Please see Appendices A and B to help you determine the most effective prospecting methods for your business, and the right way to set up the SCORE to ensure that the prospecting method is used correctly, and that the result of the prospecting method is what you want—a chance to sell your product or service to someone you think is likely to be a qualified prospect (see Chapter 4 for what it means for a prospect to be qualified).

Prospecting Objections

When you make a SCORE, one of two things will happen:

1. The person will agree to your suggestion and set up a meeting with you, or
2. The person will say that he or she does not want to meet you.

The first is great. Have your calendar ready and set a meeting.

The second is called a prospecting objection. When that happens, you have two choices: (1) accept it and move on to the next call, or (2) answer it.

If you would like to improve your success ratio, try #2. Since you don't have anything to lose (they already said no, how much worse could it get), then you should try to answer the objection, and see if you can get the meeting anyway.

Let's try an exercise to help you be more effective at this.

Close this book, and write down every objection to a request for a meeting that you have ever heard. I'll give you three to start with; see how many more you can come up with.

1. I don't have time.
2. We never had good results with that before.
3. I need to think about it.

Now close the book, and don't open it again until you have completed your list.

My List of Prospecting Objections

- I don't have time to talk to you.
- Send me something.
- We are working with someone else.
- We don't have any money in the budget.
- I am not the decision maker.
- We do that internally.

- This is not a good time for us.
- Your price is too high.
- We're not interested.
- We don't have confidence in you or your company.
- I need to think about it.
- We never had good results with that before.
- The "INDUSTRY SPECIFIC" objection

Are there any objections on your list that are not on mine? We may have used different words, but really try to see if the ones on your list match any on my list, and cross off of your list anything you see on my list. How many do you have left?

I do this exercise in many of my sales training seminars, and only one time did the group come up with an objection that was not on my pre-printed list. It was very industry specific, so I added that as the last objection—the "industry specific" objection.

So why is this relevant? Asking for a meeting is like a mini-sale within a sale, and it has its own objection phase, but in this tightly defined part of the process, the objections are very predictable, and there are not so many of them. Make it a point to come up with solid, comfortable, effective answers for each objection. Write them down and refine them with your colleagues or manager, then try them with your prospects. If you keep getting the same objections, and you have a good answer for them, you may turn around a percentage of them.

Remember, you use these objection responses after it looks like you have already lost the request for conversation battle, so even a 10 percent or 20 percent turn around rate is worth the effort, and you may even get more than that—what do you have to lose? The cost-benefit analysis is clear. One more comment from you could lead to a measurable increase in conversions at this stage of the process. Sounds like it is worth the effort, wouldn't you agree?

Most prospective clients give objections out of habit. Generally speaking, people instinctively don't like change and they don't like to put new things on their calendar, so they resist by reflex. If you can be professional and confident in the way you answer them, you will often move past the objection and sometimes even into the "win" column.

In Appendix C, I list some common responses to these prospecting objections—feel free to try some out. I hope they work well for you; they do for most of my clients.

When you go through the exercises in Appendix A, you will be directed to develop your prospecting methods to support the focused approach to prospecting described in this chapter. In Appendix B you will go through an exercise to develop your SCORE script, and in Appendix C, I provide suggested answers for some common prospecting objections. If you do all of that, you should be well positioned to start generating new business.

Remember what I mentioned at the start of the chapter? Prospecting is one of the main and most critical areas where salespeople fail. So before we move on from prospecting, let's address some of the reasons that are responsible for this key, early stage of the sales process step not happening correctly in the first place.

Prospecting is Psychologically Difficult

Imagine this:

A young single guy is sitting in a bar one night. From across the room, he sees a sweet looking, beautiful woman. She is looking at him, smiling. Her gaze lingers. She seems to be inviting him over with her eyes, but nothing else. What happens next...

If this were a novel or TV show (and I am not writing a novel or TV show), the guy would probably go over and start talking to the girl. Otherwise, there would not be a need to have this moment in the story line, unless we want to show the guy is shy, or to show some other reason he doesn't go over.

What happens in the real world a LOT of the time is this:

Quite often, the guy starts making up lots of reasons in his head about why she wouldn't really be interested in him, as a justification for not going over:

- She probably has a boyfriend—a girl that pretty surely does;
- Maybe she is looking at someone else;
- I forgot to floss my teeth and probably have bad breath;
- Etc.

Human beings don't like rejection. We will do almost anything to avoid it. Unfortunately, this also includes not trying things that could succeed, because they might fail.

Salespeople do this a lot. Some of the most fantastic examples of human creativity seem to come from salespeople finding reasons not to prospect.

The fear of avoiding prospecting comes from two things:

1. Not knowing how to do it
2. Not having reasonable expectations (HINT: you won't get meetings and make sales 100 percent of the time)

In Appendix A, B, and C, I lay out some guidelines for setting up, tracking, and succeeding with prospecting. You will need to gain competence and confidence with these skills to be successful in sales. You will not succeed with each attempt, but if you make a good effort with each attempt, have reasonable expectations, and you actually make the attempts, you will be much more successful. That will help with the first problem of not knowing how to do it.

By the way, our friend at the bar is more likely to be successful if he approaches the woman with some kind of smoothly delivered and clever "reason for the call" as well. Different kind of score, but same basic idea, right?

So what about the reasonable expectations? In the previous chapter on leads, I mentioned some of the important consequences of sticking to a plan, focusing on the execution, and doing that over a sustained period of time. I also shared some data about some of my prospecting efforts, and some different ways to look at the raw data results that those efforts produced. Having realistic expectations and a positive perspective on the outcomes you achieve will help you with the second problem. Review that part of the previous chapter now if you need to, but realize that if you won't make consistent, sustained efforts to engage prospects for new business, the rest of the process won't follow, including the ultimate goal of closing the deal.

Talking yourself out of trying is a good way to fail. Trying at least gives you a chance to succeed. Shall we try?

You Are Ready to Move on From This Step When

The prospecting stage is done when you have an agreement to communicate with someone who is a prospect, although not yet a qualified prospect. The forum in which communication occurs is not important. In some cases, you will ask for a meeting; in others, the phone conversation you are already on may simply continue; in still others, you may agree with the prospective client that another phone conversation can happen at some time in the future. According to my definition, prospecting is an attempt to request a forum for communication from someone who you believe could be a qualified prospect. Once you have reached an agreement to arrange a specific time and method for communicating about the possibility of doing business together, you have completed the prospecting stage and are ready to move on to the next step—qualification.

Review of Key Points

Chapter 3
Sales Process Step #2: Prospecting

- Prospecting is any attempt to request a forum for sales related communication from someone who you believe could be a qualified prospect.
- Prospecting is one of the main areas where most salespeople fail by not doing enough; and not doing so consistently and effectively.
- There are at least 21 prospecting methods, probably more. Everyone should be able to find one or two that work, and then work them.
- From the 21+ prospecting methods, we really only have two categories: doing something to set up an introduction call and making that introduction call without any kind of a set up (i.e., cold calling).
- The key to all introduction calls is the creation and appropriate usage of the right "reason" for the call.
- The prospecting method you choose should be executed to set up that "reason for the call" that you will use during the communication to set up the SCORE (Sales Communication Request).
- Prospecting should be directed at setting a meeting or a conversation about making a sale.
- Some people will not want to meet with you, and will offer prospecting objections.
- Prospecting objections are predictable, and should be prepared for (see Appendix B for more information).
- Prospecting is psychologically difficult, but even more so without a specific idea about how to do it and without knowing what kind of expectations are realistic.

Exercises
- Read Appendix A and identify which prospecting methods are most appropriate for you. Try to choose one or more that are proactive and one or more that take a little more time to mature. These different rhythms are important. Some will allow you to get to work

right away, while others may prove very successful, although may take some time to develop.

- Read Appendix B and develop a script applicable to each of your prospecting methods. Start by going back to each prospecting method and writing out the "reason for the call" based on the specific method. Use your own words, and practice your scripts out loud. Once they sound right, print them in large font, and read them as you call your prospects. If you practice before calling, you will not sound like you are reading, just like good actors do not sound like they are reading a script. Be sure the words are your words, and make them sound natural. It is much easier than making it up as you go along, and it will sound a lot better to your prospect (or to the person at the bar).

- Read Appendix C and re-write the responses to the prospecting objections into words that are comfortable for you. Practice saying them out loud. They will sound different when you say them than you imagine they will when you just read them. Make sure they sound right when you say them, and modify them until they do. It may feel different still when you use these with customers, so create them on a document on your computer, and modify them as you use them. You won't need to look at your document when you talk with people, but the process of writing them out will help you remember them and execute them more confidently.

CHAPTER 4

Sales Process Step #3: Qualification

Definition of Qualification

Qualification is the process of confirming that the person you are communicating with is both ABLE TO and LIKELY TO say YES to your offer.

Some Thoughts About the Qualification Step in the Process

Qualification should be the first thing that happens when you are done with prospecting and into a sales conversation with a prospective client. Some of the elements of qualification might have happened during prospecting, but the timing is not as important as the idea that before doing needs analysis, qualification should be completed.

So what does it mean to be "able to" and "likely to" say "yes" to your offer? This is not to say that you need to get a pre-commitment to agree (although it is OK if you do). However, you want to identify at least three things about your prospect before you continue trying to move into the next steps of the process:

- Is this person the decision maker?
- Is there "pain" that needs to be alleviated?
- Is there a budget to fix the source of the pain, insofar as your company may offer a solution?
- Are there some industry or company specific criteria that need to be met in order to consider the prospect qualified *(optional, if needed)*?

If you can get an affirmative answer to these questions, then the person you are talking to is both able to say yes (is the decision maker, and has the money for your solution), and likely to say yes (has some form of pain that your product or service can alleviate). That doesn't mean that they will, but the absence of any one of these elements greatly increases the likelihood that a sale will not happen. This is why you MUST establish them before moving too far into the sales process, wasting valuable time and energy that you could rather direct at a qualified prospect. Selling to unqualified prospects is a losers' game. You just can't win, so find out early if the game is worth playing, then play hard or move on accordingly.

Working with Decision Makers

You must realize this: if there are one hundred people in a company, then one hundred of them can say "no" to you. The janitor can say no, the secretary can say no, the summer intern can say no.

On the other hand, only a few, and maybe even only one person in the company can say yes to your sales offer. Qualification is about making sure that you are talking to one or all of the people who can say yes, and finding out if they are likely to do so.

For some reason, people will make meetings with you even if they cannot make an affirmative decision about your product or service. If you don't figure this out before you go through the entire sales process, your overall efficiency will be dramatically reduced. You must understand the decision-making apparatus of the organization you are trying to sell to, and if at all possible, be in direct contact with the decision maker(s) throughout your sales process. You can be successful if you break this rule, but your work will be a LOT more difficult.

Contrary to the fears of many salespeople, working with decision makers is a joy. When you work with decision makers, you realize that, quite often, the reason they are the ones in a position of power is that they are capable of making judgments for the good of the company. As such, if you are able to identify needs (step 4 in the process) and propose solutions that work well for them (step 5 in the process), then you will be able to move the sales process forward because decision makers CAN act on these issues. No one else can. Period.

On the other hand, people who meet with you that can't say yes make your meetings and your efforts to sell miserable. Since they can't say yes, they keep you jumping from one irrelevant thing to another, in order to hide the fact that they are not able to make the decision. You might see lots of new objections, lots of requests for information, modifications to the proposal, and so forth. This keeps them from having to admit that they can't make a decision, and worst of all, it keeps you from getting to a decision—with them or with other prospects with whom you could be spending this time and energy. As sales professionals, we need to figure out quickly if we are talking to the right people or not; and the right people are those who can say yes!

Selling Pain Relief

The best business you can be in is the pain relief business. If you are selling aspirin and your client has a headache, your job will be easy. Accordingly, if you want to make your job easy, whatever you sell, help your client to identify early in the process the specific pain that your product or service can alleviate. It does not have to be in great detail at this stage of the game—you can save that for the needs analysis stage—but to consider someone as qualified, you should know that there is some kind of pain that you can fix for them.

I know that pain is a strong word. I used it for that reason. Identifying problems or needs is nice. That means you can talk about something relevant. You can and will make some sales if you identify problems and needs. On the other hand, if you talk to decision makers, and make them see the pain they are in that you can fix, your effectiveness will increase dramatically. You will make more sales, and make them more easily.

Budget

The job we are talking about is sales. We defined a salesperson as the person who convinces someone in another company to transfer money to their company, so at some point, we should talk about money! In the spirit of front loading—and, more directly, in the spirit of not going through the rest of the process only to find out that the client does not have the money—we need to establish general guidelines around budget early on as a part of the qualification phase.

Be careful not to go overboard. In many cases, a careful needs analysis will be required in order to know exactly what the client needs and exactly how much that might cost, but a detailed needs analysis can often require a lot of time, money and energy, so start with establishing a general range of comfort around the budget requirements of your offering and the client's need.

After identifying pain at the general level, you can say something like, *"Well, in my experience, there is a wide range of solutions that can fix these issues. Although we'll need to learn a lot more details before suggesting a specific solution, the typical solution is closer to five figures than four. Is it going to make sense to do some detailed needs analysis if we know that the final price will be in the tens of thousands of dollars?"*

Getting an affirmative answer to even a question this general will help a lot when it comes time to close. Getting a negative answer will surely save you a lot of time and trouble at the closing phase—you now know that it is not worth the time and effort to get there and to fight. Think of all of the trouble you just saved yourself.

The Industry Specific Qualification

Many of the companies I work with have some additional specific information they need to get before moving on to needs analysis. I can't address those here; you probably know what they are for your own situation. So add that to the three qualifications above if it is applicable.

Mutual Qualification

It can be useful to think about qualification as a two-way street. A good term for this might be *mutual* qualification. What can you do to qualify yourself to the prospect at this stage of the game?

What you should NOT do is present. If you want to put your client to sleep, open the meeting with a long presentation about the history of your company and all of the great things that the company has done since it opened its doors several decades ago. Unless the client asks for this, don't do it! Think about the sales process as a conversation between two people on a stage. The spotlight shines on the person who is the subject of the conversation. You are selling when the spotlight is on them, and you are working to identify their situation so that you can solve their problem. The accomplishments of your company founder don't have a place there.

So what can you do to qualify yourself to the prospect at this stage of the game? Two simple things set the framework.

Do what we have discussed already
Be focused and directed in your efforts to set up the meeting. Open the meeting by making sure that the time invested in working together makes sense for both of you. If you are talking to a decision maker, they will consciously or subconsciously recognize this professionalism on your part. Without doing anything specific, your behaviors and demeanor will qualify you as someone who is focused and deliberate about your time. This will be recognized, and will help you. This is not to say that you need to be manic, but rather, deliberate. You are not there to waste anybody's time, and you are being deliberate about making sure that you don't.

Be the first to suggest getting down to business
The few minutes between the moment you make eye contact with your prospect and the moment when you start talking about business will be filled with some light "small" talk. It just doesn't make sense to start your sales conversation in the lobby, as you walk down the hall to the conference room, or before you sit down and take out your note pad. Just be careful not to let this time go too long, and be sure that you don't chat so much as to make the prospect feel compelled to say, *"OK, so let's get down to business."*

This puts you on the defensive. It is not a big problem, but one you should avoid. Get a feel for the timing, and when it feels like time to get started with the business discussion, suggest that you get started, and prove yet again that you are a professional who respects the time of your client, as well as your own time. It is the right message to send.

NOTE: This advice is perfect in the US, and most of Europe, but may not be applicable in all countries. Many business cultures have become accustomed to the "let's get down to business" style of American business people, but be careful. It may seem aggressive depending on the culture, the nature of the sale and the relationship between the parties. I can't provide guidance for all possibilities here, but if you are working internationally, do be sure to get some input about the specific culture within which you are working.

You Are Ready to Move on From This Step When

You are ready to move into the next stage of the selling process when you know the following things:

- Am I talking to someone who can say "yes"?
- Is there pain?
- Is there a budget to fix the pain?
- Is there an industry or company specific qualifier that needs to be recognized and confirmed?

Once you know these things, you are ready to start needs analysis, unless you want to take a shortcut (see the next chapter for that).

Review of Key Points

Chapter 4
Sales Process Step #3: Qualification

- Qualification is the process of confirming that the person you are communicating with is both ABLE TO and LIKELY TO say YES to your offer.
- Failure to qualify properly before moving further into the sales process is risking an investment of your time in a prospect that has no real likelihood of buying from you. The cost for you is the opportunity cost: not being able to use that same time to engage in the selling process with someone else who is qualified to buy from you. Qualify well and early to avoid this fate.
- Qualification is a function of at least four elements:
  1. Ensuring that you are talking to the decision maker(s);
  2. Ensuring that there is some "pain" that your product or service can alleviate;
  3. Ensuring that there is money in the budget to buy your solution;
  4. Anything that might be an industry specific requirement.
- It is never too early to qualify yourself to the prospect. Do this by:
  1. Not presenting before qualification and needs analysis;
  2. Be professional, focused and directed in your efforts leading up to and including qualification;
  3. Be the first person in your meetings to suggest that you move from small talk to a business related discussion—don't make them ask you to stop talking about your hobbies.

Exercises
- Make a list of the things you need to know from your prospects before you can consider them qualified. Your list should include information about decision-making status, budget, and pain. Be sure to include any industry specific, company specific, or legal requirements that need to be met as well.

- Consider your own sales efforts in the past. How many times have you entered into the sales process without qualifying well? What has that cost you in terms of time and the opportunity to generate new lines of business elsewhere with other, more qualified prospects? If you have ever faced the "we don't have the budget for that" objection after an extensive needs analysis and the presentation of your proposal, then you failed to address budget in the qualification stage. Are there other examples like this in your sales history? Think about them now, and strategize about how to resolve them earlier in the sales process in the future.

- Have you tried to qualify yourself by presenting? Can you see how this may not be the best way to earn trust and to establish rapport? What can you do to qualify yourself to the prospect early in the sales process instead of doing so by presenting? Consider specific ways that you can demonstrate that you are professional, and specific ways that you can demonstrate expertise in your field. Make sure you can do so without presenting, such as managing the time flow of the meeting, and asking great questions in the right order to lead you down the right path towards the early stages of a sale. Make a list, and be specific.

CHAPTER 5

Process Shortcut #1: The Mini-Contract

This chapter describes the first of two "process shortcuts," the mini-contract. This may or may not be directly applicable to your sales process. It is not mandatory. However, if you can find a way to adapt the principles of the mini-contract into your sales methodology, it can be a powerful sales process accelerator.

I give full credit where credit is due, and the mini-contract method is something I learned from a client named Gabor Kornai. At the time, he was running and I was consulting at one of the largest management consulting firms in Hungary.

In the normal course of my work with his company, I asked Gabor a question I have asked every client I have worked with since 2005: *"Please describe your sales process to me."* The typical answer is usually a convoluted mess that has no consistency whatsoever—a few words about why a sales process is not appropriate for their particular style of business, an overture to some random examples of how they once fell into a client meeting, yada, yada, yada, and then I write a proposal, and sometimes they agree.

In other words, these typical answers translated into an admission of no process at all. Rather, like a blind pig, occasional food is found through random effort, and success remains at the level of one's peers, like-minded blind pigs digging for business development truffles in the darkness of unfocused and unpolished effort.

But not Gabor.

I didn't even need to give him the almost universally requested explanation of what I meant by sales process—a stalling tactic if I ever saw one. Gabor, typical of one who knew the answer based on his ownership of the material, just answered. His answer went something like this:

"Once I have a meeting, I simply dig for pain. If the client does not have some kind of pain, then there is nothing for me to fix."

NOTE: The use of the word pain is not a coincidence, we just both happen to use it for the same reason and in the same context. I found that to be interesting.

Once the pain has been found, then Gabor instantly suggests what he calls a mini-contract. Why is this so revolutionary? Gabor is in the IT consulting business. Most of the non-business related consultants I work with (environmental, IT, etc.) are great technicians and very bad salespeople. Their instinct upon discovering a client need is to write a proposal. Proposal writing can be time consuming in the IT consulting business, and is usually very detail intensive. It is also usually done for free, and it is not a great tool to use to secure a deal, if the project for which the proposal is being written is not properly qualified before the proposal is written and delivered—more on this later in the process.

Since technical consultants are not usually good salespeople and they do not typically do a good job of qualifying, the failure rate on these proposals is high.

Did you catch that—time consuming proposals written by expensive, technical consultants with a high failure rate? No wonder Gabor had grey hair and no wonder he hired me.

Gabor's personal approach—the mini-contract—was different. Once he found the pain, he said to the prospective client something like this:

"Based on what we have discussed so far, neither of us knows how big this project is going to be, and neither of us knows if we actually want to work on it together. Accordingly, I suggest the following. I think that we can do a preliminary needs analysis in about two weeks. This will require some people from my company to work with some people from your company to develop the specifications. At the end

of the two weeks, we will have a detailed document to help us define the scope of our work together, and our people will have some experience working together—at least enough to decide if it looks promising enough to continue."

"So why don't we each pay for a week. We will do two weeks of work, you pay us for one—that way we each contribute a week's worth of resources to help us make this decision to work together in a more informed manner. Does that sound OK to you?"

If the client says no, then Gabor surmises that he or she probably was never serious, and a proposal written for free probably would not have been approved. He believes in his ability to find the pain, and once he does, he tests whether or not it is real, using this method. So if the client says "no" after the pain has been identified, this is a positive outcome, in that it saves the time of writing a cost intensive proposal that is likely destined for rejection.

If the client says yes, then the needs analysis, which is normally free, is partially paid for—also a good outcome, but that is not the best part. Two other important things happen here.

First, the client who works through the two-week mini-contract diagnosis has more buy-in than one who receives a free proposal. After working together for two weeks and spending some money, the least likely outcome is that the mini-contract will define work that goes to another consulting firm.

The second least likely outcome is that no work is done. If pain was discovered during qualification, then two weeks' worth of detailed needs analysis will almost certainly validate that pain. Based on that, and the aforementioned buy-in, the client is likely to move forward in solving the problem. As such, the most likely outcome is that the project moves forward, especially since the mini-contract is laser focused on finding as many potential areas of opportunity as possible for the consulting firm.

The delivery of the results of the mini-contract is often a litany of problems, followed by a calm assurance that these have been prioritized, and that a fraction of the issues that were identified can be leveraged to fix a majority of the problems—classic consultative selling.

So what can you use as your mini-contract? If you sell any kind of complex service, then any kind of a detailed diagnosis will work. If you are selling any kind of physical product, then any kind of a free trial period can act as a mini-contract for you. This has been referred to as the puppy dog-style close, and it is a form of mini-contract if the "puppy" represents a small portion of the total sale or a trial period.

NOTE: The phrase "puppy dog close" comes from the idea that a pet store owner can sell a lot of puppies if he interrupts the inevitable argument between parent and child when the child is whining to buy the puppy in the pet store and the parent says no. The savvy pet store owner can suggest that they take the puppy home for a week to see if they want to keep him. How many puppies come back to the store? Probably not too many, but I am sure that the new dog owners will be back to the friendly pet store for supplies.

If you can find a mini-contract for diagnosis or some other preliminary piece of work together, or a puppy dog style trial period in your offering, then you can effectively close at step 3 in the 7 step sales process. How is that for efficient? This is a great example of front loading—finishing a seven-step process in three steps.

Review of Key Points

Chapter 5
Process Shortcut #1: The Mini-Contract

- A mini-contract is a way to get paid to do some form of needs analysis or preliminary work with a client.
- If you make finding pain the last part of your qualification (meaning that you qualified on all other qualification factors first), then you are ready to suggest a mini-contract once pain has been identified.
- Your offer of a mini-contract can be at a normal price, or at some kind of a discount, based on your preference and industry tolerance.
- In some cases, a mini-contract is not possible, but some kind of detailed diagnostic process should be utilized before a full proposal is made (see Chapter 6 on Needs Analysis).
- A detailed, cooperative diagnostic processes will help to ensure a sale by generating buy-in, as well as a very thorough proposal to address a very well-defined problem.
- The puppy dog close is another form of mini-contract. Allow a trial usage to help secure the sale.
- The main take away from the mini-contract discussion is that it is a good use of your time to consider your own selling situation and try to find some smaller something you can offer, do, or sell in order to set up a more robust and easily closable sale at the end of the mini-contract period.

Exercises
- Identify the kinds of mini-contracts that might be applicable to your selling situation. Is there some kind of detailed diagnostic that you can offer, one which you can split the cost with your client? This works well for consultative selling and complex sales situations. Is there something you can let them test for a week, like the puppy dog close? This works well for pieces of equipment, software, subscriptions, and of course puppy dogs.
- If you can identify something in your business around which you can use the mini-contract method, how will you set it up? What

question do you need to ask and how should it be answered in a way that you can suggest the mini-contract?

- If you are splitting the cost of something to establish the mini-contract, do you need approval from your manager to do so? How can you justify that? Come up with a plan before you approach your manager. Perhaps you can suggest some kind of a test (use the mini-contract to get internal approval for the mini-contract).

CHAPTER 6

Sales Process Step #4: Needs Analysis

Definition of Needs Analysis

Needs analysis is the part of the sales process in which you learn in detail what the prospective client needs to fix by means of something your company might be able to provide.

Some Thoughts About the Needs Analysis Step in the Process

Whether you do the needs analysis as a mini-contract and get paid for it, or you simply ask the questions you need to ask as a part of the sales process in advance of any kind of a close, needs analysis is a central, critical part of the sales process. If you are indeed working with a qualified candidate, then the work you do in this stage will determine your potential for success or failure in your attempt to secure the deal you are after. If you don't know what the client needs, how can you make a compelling offer?

In the qualification step, we talked about identifying pain. In needs analysis, we need graphic details about that pain, the source of the pain, and the elements of a desired solution for alleviating that pain from the perspective of the prospective client. Here, you want to think about yourself as a doctor, a diagnostician.

To be a successful diagnostician, a doctor must have thorough knowledge of all basic body systems and diseases and a firm grasp on treatment options, including surgery, medication, and various therapies. He does not need to be a pharmacist, a surgeon, or otherwise capable of delivering these remedies, but he needs to know enough to make recommendations and referrals that are appropriate for the identified needs of his patient. He uses this knowledge to ask questions that narrow down the possible causes of the pain of his patient, so that he can prescribe the correct treatment.

In other words, a good diagnostician needs to be a subject matter expert. We covered the importance of expertise in chapter 1. This is the part of the sales process where that expertise is most evident and most critical.

Like the diagnosing doctor, you don't need to be able to deliver the cure for your client's pain, but you do need to know how to help clarify the pain, and then point out the best solution options. Many prospective clients have pain, but do not know the source. It is also possible that they think they know the source, but are wrong. Remember our sales mindset? You are the expert here. Your clients most likely have recent experience in only their own company, while you have seen many companies struggle with similar issues, address them with assorted attempts to fix the problems, and have a variety of results coming from these attempts. Remember this, and remind your prospective client of this. You are the expert! The expert is here to help!

If you can ask the right questions, you may be able to help your clients find a better solution to their problem than the one they thought they should try. If you do, chances are better than good that they will buy from you. In this case, you are no longer a salesperson, but a problem solver, a consultant, a real asset for the client. You are not only offering a product or service, but you also help the client understand how to apply your product or service to meet some pressing need and to relieve the pain that may not have been fully understood before you came along to help.

The specific elements of a needs analysis will be different for each industry and each project. This book can't cover the parts of needs analysis that are specific to your company, industry, country, and so on. As such, it is incumbent upon you to understand fully what needs you must uncover from your client in your own situation, and you should have a systematic methodology for getting to those needs. It will make the difference between fighting for an order and establishing the kinds of client relationships that ensure current and possibly future business opportunities, as the case may be, for your specific situation.

As an example, let's look at my work as a sales consultant. In this case, the methodology looks like this:

First, I confirm with the client at the start of our first meeting that we are meeting because there is some kind of improvement that the client would like to see in his or her sales organization. In other words, I ask if that is true:

"So, since you wanted to meet with me, a sales consultant, can I assume that this means that there is some part of your sales organization that you would like me to help you improve?"

If this is not true, then I need to know why they want to meet with me, a sales consultant. If it is true, it is an affirmation of this key element of the qualification—they have pain, and they may want me to help fix it. Now we need to clarify it, and establish my credentials as the right provider of treatment.

Second, I ask them to tell me about the areas in their sales organization that they would like to improve. I ask LOTS of questions, suggest trial solutions (see below), and dig into assumptions whenever I can.

By asking good questions, I demonstrate that I have a good command of the subject matter. If I do this well, then by the end of this stage, I have fully qualified myself to the prospective client as a good resource. No one will buy sales consulting from me unless I can show that I know my material, and am a better salesperson than their best salespeople. This is where that can really happen for me. If you are an expert in your field, then you will also be able to ask the kinds of questions that not only help you understand the issues facing the client, but simultaneously help the client see that you are a master of the subject matter with which they need your help; a bit of a win-win situation here.

Asking good questions also allows me to make a list of sales-related issues that need to be solved. This is the specific pain that the client feels. You will do the same, in the subject matter that is relevant to the conversation you are having with your client.

Once I believe that I have a good list of issues, I read them back to the client.

"So it sounds like the following are the key issues in your sales organization (read the list). Have we missed anything?"

Third, I suggest that each of the issues raises several currently unanswerable questions about the organization and the people in it, and I state the questions I think we need to answer in order to uncover the root causes of the issues we just identified. Once I can get agreement on the list of the right, currently unanswerable questions, then closing a mini-contract for a more thorough diagnostic process is an obvious next step.

The mini-contract for diagnosis is great, because I get paid to flesh out the true sources of pain and it leads to lots of consulting, training, and coaching revenue for me. It is a good set up for me, and it serves the needs of the client. Together we identify the problems in his or her sales organization, and then set out to fix them. Everybody wins.

It sounds simple and obvious, but it took me some time to realize that this is the best approach for me. I finally got there by reverse engineering:

1. I asked myself what I wanted (a mini-contract for diagnosis).
2. I realized that the diagnosis answers key questions, so to get a contract for the diagnosis, I needed to identify and get agreement on the currently unanswerable questions with the client.
3. I realized that the questions derive from specific sales issues in the organization, and the need to understand their root causes.
4. And, as a point of departure, prospective clients meet with me because they have issues in their sales organizations that they want to solve.

Once I took these four things and turned them around, I had my needs analysis methodology, as illustrated in the example that preceded the numbered list above. To develop this for your own situation, start with the most successful end to a qualification, needs analysis meeting, or set of meetings. What do you want to learn, know, do, or agree to with your client that will set you up for success in the later parts of the sales process (proposal, objections and negotiations, and closing the deal)? What will set that up in the clients' mind in the most convincing way?

In most cases, your needs analysis methodology will be most effective if it helps to show prospective clients those of their pains which are not fully understood (mini-contract for further diagnosis) or that can be resolved by your solution (proposal, objections, and close). Work with your manager and your colleagues or with an outside coach or consultant to develop this methodology. If you develop and execute it well, it can and will pay off big time for you.

Universal Elements of Needs Analysis

Beyond the industry, company, and salesperson specific elements of needs analysis, there are also some universal elements of the needs analysis step in the process. Let's talk about those now.

Rapport, Trust, Differentiation, and Credibility

Have you ever met someone at a party and had a conversation that was mostly you answering their questions about you? You may not have been aware of it during or immediately after the conversation, but at some point in time, you realize that you spoke for 20 minutes, and you know nothing about them. It started with some witty comment about something, then it was on to what you do for a living, where you traveled on vacation, what book you are reading and why you think it is important.

In spite of your later realization, the first thing you probably thought when you disengaged from the conversation was something like:

- What a nice person!
- What a smart person!
- What an interesting person!

Only later did you realize that you did all of the talking and that your initial conclusions were based on how they made you feel, not on what they said.

Needs analysis is a great vehicle, not only to learn about the needs of the client, but also to establish your credibility, to earn the trust of the client, and to differentiate yourself from your competition, all while establishing a rapport that you can build on as the relationship and the sales process progresses.

Do you remember our discussion about being an industry expert? This is the time to show that, but not with a fancy PowerPoint presentation or an award-winning monologue. Rather, demonstrate your expertise by asking good questions, probing, and working hard to understand the client's needs. In this way, you will have the opportunity to show how much you know, how interested you are in the client and in his situation, how trustworthy you can be, and how different you are from other "typical" salespeople or consultants that the prospect may have met with at some other time. As discussed above, this helps in identifying the pain, which will help you make the right proposal and close it, but of equal importance, it will establish you as the trusted resource they are looking for. There is bit of overlap here, but that is OK. Asking questions of a qualified prospect helps in all of the right ways—develop the expertise to execute this well, and the rest of your job will be much easier.

I tell my kids that, as often as not, being smart is not about having the answers; rather, it is about asking the right questions. It is true for sales professionals as well.

Why the customer is going to buy from you?

Wouldn't it be great if we were the only game in town—the only source of what our clients need? Well, in most cases, this is not true. So how do we deal with that? I believe firmly in never saying anything bad about the competition, but I believe even more in never mentioning the competition at all. You do need to know and understand your competitors so that you can position yourself against them, just not by name. Rather, work to understand the purchase criteria, and use that information plus your knowledge of your competitors to highlight your relative strengths.

Most prospective clients are not so deliberate as to spell out their purchase criteria in concrete terms. Often, it can just be price, rapport, reputation of the firm, or how professionally organized the proposal is. If the right combination of these factors are in your favor, you're in luck. But it is luck.

A better approach is to work with the client to define the important factors driving the purchase decision. If these are known to you, or better still, suggested by you to the client as you probe the issue, you can work to emphasize these factors into the presentation of your company (HINT: try to suggest those where you are strongest). If the decision criteria are known to you and you know that there is no way you will win, since known competition is MUCH stronger than you in a certain key criterion, you can address it with the client and determine if it makes sense to continue.

Most importantly, you create a more rational decision making environment. Once the drivers of the purchase decision are out in the open, the client will be less likely to favor the blue report cover to the red, or the attractive salesperson to the less attractive one. Rather, the client will look at the proposal from the perspective of what meets his needs. If you are doing a good job of needs analysis, and you also understand these decision driving criteria, you can better position yourself to win.

How will the decision be made to buy from you?

"How the decision will be made to buy from you" sounds a lot like the last section heading, "why the customer will buy from you," but it is not. HOW is about the decision-making dynamics within the company. If you don't know them, then you are working uphill.

The day I wrote the first draft of this section, I had placed a call to the CEO of a small software firm. I had met with him a month prior. At the time, we had a ninety-minute meeting where I qualified him as the decision maker (he was not completely truthful), all of the needs were explored, and a solution developed and priced out, so I attempted to close. I was told that for this $3000 decision that was critical to the success of the sales team, the CEO had to check with the other owner.

Deferral to the rest of the decision making team is hard to overcome on the spot, so I did what I could, and asked him whether if it was only up to him, would he move forward. He said, "Yes." There was only one other decision maker, so I was at least 50 percent confident in a success.

A week later, I called him, and he told me that he had discussed it with the other owner, who, by the way, was his wife. He then told me that *they* had decided to do only the first phase of the project, as a starting point, for only $1000. I told him that it was a good start, and I sent him a revised proposal, thinking the next step was scheduling delivery of the services.

A few days later, I called him, and he told me that *they* had decided that even this smaller proposal was too much money; there was no value. This was a long way from the agreement at the end of the personal meeting with the CEO for the aforementioned "critical" $3000 proposal.

The point is this: I assumed that the CEO could make a decision, partly due to his title, and partly due to his affirmation of his ability to do so. I did not know how the decision would be made, and I lost because of it. It is entirely possible that the CEO was the sole decision maker, and he made up an imaginary partner as a way to say no to me. Even in this case the failure was that I did not clarify this in the early stages of qualification.

To the extent that you can, you need to learn who will be involved in the decision, and you need to make efforts to sell to them yourself. Selling by proxy is not nearly as likely to succeed as the more direct methods.

In order to find out who will be involved in the decision making and to include them in the sales meeting(s), start by asking in the prospecting phase. After you set up the meeting, ask if there is anyone else who might want to learn more about your product or service directly from you before the decision is made. Confirm the same thing again in your first meeting, during the qualification step. But by all means, reconfirm here in the needs analysis step.

Beyond the direct approach, asking who will be involved in the decision, there is an indirect approach that can supplement your direct questions. As you learn about the more detailed elements of your proposal, you should know from your experience what are the various roles in the company that are involved in the decision. Ask about them. Are there any partners who might need more information? Does the board need to be involved in a decision this large, and if so, would it make sense to have you present to them? YOU are the salesperson. Put yourself in a position where you can do the selling if you want it to be done right.

Stakeholders

Stakeholders are people who are affected by a decision, although they may not be decision makers. It is important to identify them, assess their needs, and make sure that they are on board. It will be hard for your decision maker(s) to sell your idea internally when the time comes to implement unless they know in advance that these stakeholders are on board.

Stakeholders should be easy to find, since you, as an expert on your product, know how it was implemented for most of your previous clients. Ask about the job titles that usually get involved after the sale is complete, and ask your decision maker if it makes sense to get input from those people during the pre-sales processes. It may or may not work, but if it does, you may well have more of these decision influencers on your side before the final decision is made, and more information from them with which to create a winning solution. Both of those things will bode well for you.

Budget

Budget was an element of qualification, and it shows up again here in needs analysis. In the qualification stage, we wanted to know whether, in general terms, there is money available to pay for our rough estimate of the total cost of our products and/or services. In the needs analysis phase, two additional levels of clarity are required.

First, as you begin to identify needs at a greater level of detail than you did in the qualification step, it may become clear that your initial rough estimate was too low. You need to address this now or you will sabotage the efforts you made in qualification. Prospects will remember the numbers you talked about early, and if they change in the proposal, especially if they change significantly and in an upwards direction, it won't be well received.

You can address this immediately by suggesting something like, *"Hmmm, it wasn't clear to me from our initial discussion that X and Y would also need to be addressed. This is going to significantly revise the total estimate of the cost, should we talk about that now or should we complete the needs analysis before talking about the price?"*

The second element of budget that you will want to address in the needs analysis phase is where the money will come from. Salespeople often make the mistake of seeing the company as having a single budget. When a client says, "We don't have room for this in the budget," the salesperson imagines one big soup kettle from which the money comes. The client, on the other hand, may imagine a buffet table, with your services coming from one specific bowl, which may or may not be empty. It may be worthwhile to help your client consider how to think about your products and services as applicable to multiple "budget bowls," so that one of the bowls might help to support another if need be.

For example, among other things, I sell recruiting services for salespeople. It can be argued in some organizations that sales recruiting should be, at least in part, applied to the marketing budget. The logic goes something like this:

The job of marketing is to generate leads that can be converted. The job is not done until conversion happens. Toward this end, there is a handoff from marketing to sales that is critical. It must happen while the leads are fresh, and they must be contacted quickly and professionally by the sales team in order to make them most likely to convert. As such, it can be argued that sales and marketing should split the budget for recruiting entry-level salespeople for follow up, rather than putting that budget solely on the sales department. The result is more salespeople, faster contact of the leads generated by marketing efforts, and a more robust and accurate accounting of lead conversions, as well as a more effective sales-generation effort as a result of the efforts of marketing.

If you can get your client to be more creative about how they think about your services, then you will have more bowls to scoop money from on the budget buffet table, and a higher likelihood that at least one or more of them will have enough cash to support your proposal.

Value

The remedy for the price objection is to sell value. If this is news to you, explore this concept. It is critical. There are many places where you can read about how to sell value, it is rightfully a hot topic is sales literature. What is not so often made clear is how.

To sell the value of your offering as a justification for price, you must know what the prospective client finds valuable. In this context, value is a derivative of pain. If pain is the reason you are having a conversation about fixing something, then value is the tangible, preferably quantifiable benefit set or improvement that the client will get as a result of working with you.

During needs analysis, what is important is that you learn what these quantifiable benefits are for the prospect. This should not be confused with why the customer will buy from you. That is about how the client differentiates between vendors. Uncovering value in this stage is discovering *What Is in It for the Prospect*, and will help you close the deal because you will know just what buttons to push to get that ink on the contract.

In other words, if we fix the pain, what does the client gain? If the potential gain is a quantifiable cost savings or revenue improvement worth 10 times your fee in the first year, then the decision to move ahead is a no-brainer. If the value is difficult to demonstrate to the client, it will be equally difficult to convince them to let go of any money at all.

Here is an example: I was meeting with the Managing Director of a country office of a consulting firm. He had been to one of my seminars, and asked to meet with me the following week. During our discussion, I learned that the main office was putting pressure on him to increase revenue from his office, and he did not know how to improve sales performance in his organization. He and his staff were technical consultants, and had no experience with sales or sales management, yet they needed to affect change in this area. His pain was an inability to fulfill the request of his bosses at the parent company. My services were the solution that relieved that pain. The value was clear, although not necessarily quantifiable in this case.

Or a personal example: My wife and I bought a water filter for our home. It cost a few hundred dollars, which seemed like a lot of money when we thought about it as a single expense. However, when we compared that cost plus the cost of the replacement filters against the cost of bottled water and the cost of the filters in the carafe style water filter we used at home, the economics made sense. Add to that the subjective benefits of better tasting, healthier water for us and our children, which it is, and the knowledge that we are no longer adding our own plastic bottles to a global pollution problem, and you have plenty of value to offset the price, and the perceived pain of letting go of a large lump sum of money. When the lump sum of money is counter-balanced by value, which by definition is important to the buyer, then the purchase becomes and investment rather than an expense.

The examples are simple, but clear. In each situation, the problem could be fixed by the product or service that the sales person offered in order to fix it, and the value of the solution was greater than the price.

This may seem like a short section on what is arguably one of the most important elements of the sales process. However, volumes have been written about value, but not necessarily with any substance.

My advice? Keep it simple.

Value to the client is the extent to which the alleviation of pain is worth the time, energy, and money to acquire. The more you can identify pain, the more value your proposal has to the client. If you don't identify pain, you talk price. If you identify and can relieve pain, the value of your proposal is clear. Your job is to help the client see this. It is not a small task, but it is clear. It is the core of needs analysis as discussed above. Work with your colleagues, your manager, or a consultant to develop some kind of value calculation methodology to use with the clients, and then master it.

One other thought about value selling versus price selling. Feel free to use this with your clients if they are having trouble seeing anything but price:

No one buys anything on price alone!

When the average person buys a cup of coffee, a shirt or a car, how often do they make efforts to buy the least expensive choice at the expense of all other factors? Practically never! Starbucks is not the cheapest cup of coffee. Many people even get free coffee in their office, but they still go to Starbucks. People buy a shirt because it fits well, looks nice, feels good, and is easy to care for. Many, many car choices exist beyond the cheapest base models, and people do buy these more expensive cars every day.

Obvious stuff, I know. But here are everyday purchases that are based on factors other than price. Something is more important to the buyers of these products than the price difference between the cheapest possible option and the more expensive options they choose. If you can identify the important factors for your prospective client with respect to what you are selling, then the conversation moves away from price, and into the right solution for the problem. This is value; much more fun to sell this way than on price.

Some salespeople argue that this way of thinking does not apply to corporate purchases, where price is the only factor. If you believe this to be true, then you are not talking to decision makers. Decision makers usually have a number of factors to keep in mind when making a purchase related to the problem they want to solve. Non-decision makers report to decision makers with purchase criteria, but if they don't know them all, they will focus only price and obvious issues. Talk to the decision makers to find the true sources of pain, then you can sell the value in any environment.

Some salespeople insist that they sell commodity products, and that price is the only variable. I don't believe it. Packaging, availability, financing, quality, reliability, warranty, there are many things you can find to be differentiators above and beyond the product itself. Get creative, find out what is important to the client, then sell the value!

Trial Solutions

One of the most effective things that you can do as you proceed through the needs analysis questions is to inject some trial closes. Here is how it works—I will show you how to use this trial solutions to close earlier in the process in the next section.

As you ask your needs analysis questions and stumble across opportunities, insert small comments about potential solutions to the part of the problem that you are discussing. Let me illustrate with an example.

YOU: It sounds like you are concerned about capacity problems?
PROSPECT: Yes, if we move forward as we discussed, it would really strain our operations group in the ball bearing factory.

YOU: Yes, I understand. We had another client with a similar problem; we found that for them, we could bridge the gap by contracting the work out until we could ramp up their internal capacity to meet demand. Do you think this might be an approach that we could consider to help solve this piece of the problem?

The last sentence, the off-the-cuff suggestion, is an example of a trial close. It is a simple, un-detailed, categorical suggestion of a potential approach to a problem uncovered in needs analysis. By asking trial closes, you accomplish a few key things.

1. If the client rejects the idea, then you can ask why and learn a lot about why the client thinks it may not work, and what might work better. This will help you better understand the need and the client. Try not to float too many trial closes that are rejected, as this may diminish the perception of your expertise. Once you ask a few, you probably have enough information to understand the problem, and your trial closes will come more easily into focus as the dialogue continues—so don't worry about a few misses, these really help you to clarify the thinking of both you and the client.

2. If the client likes the idea, move on without going into too much detail, but make note. This will help you in later stages. By referring back to something the client agreed to as a solution, you gain momentum behind the idea, and you set up the proposal stage for success well before you get there.

The example above is a simple one. The dialogue would be more detailed both before and after this simple example first comes up, such as going into more details about how the outsourcing might work or what issues might come up with that. At this stage, you want to keep the focus on exploring the problem, not on solving it, but putting out feelers like this will help you scope the problem more effectively, and will certainly help when it comes time to propose your solution to the problem.

You Are Ready to Move on From This Step When

When you think you are ready to move on from this step, ask the client whether he agrees with you. Say something like:

"So it looks to me like these are the issues that we might be able to help you with (list the issues in bullet point like format), is that everything?"

You are ready to move on to the next stage of the process when the client agrees with that statement. If they don't agree, then get more information and ask again when you think you have it all. Only when they agree can you move forward.

Review of Key Points

Chapter 6
Sales Process Step #4: Needs Analysis

- Needs analysis is the part of the sales process when you learn in detail what the prospective client needs to fix by means of something your company might be able to provide.

- Proper needs analysis will have tremendous influence on your ability to make and close an appropriate proposed solution to the client's needs.

- The proper perspective for effective needs analysis is that of a diagnostician. Think of yourself as a doctor asking questions in order to identify a problem you can solve. Realize that you should know your product, your client's product, your competition, and all other related material, just as you expect a doctor to know about the human body, disease, medication, and other related material.

- It is incumbent upon you to make your needs analysis systematic. This is an iterative process, so start with a model and a concept, and refine it as you go, probably for the rest of your career.

- Create your first needs analysis system model by reverse engineering back from what you want with respect to needs analysis (i.e., some agreement to move forward with a proposal based on the right information—this can be a proposal for a mini-contract or a proposal based on your needs analysis, depending on your industry and other factors specific to your situation).

- There are some elements of needs analysis that are not industry specific, and which you should try to address along with your industry specific issues. These elements are:
    1. Rapport, trust, differentiation and credibility
    2. Why the customer is going to buy from you
    3. How the decision will be made to buy from you
    4. Stakeholders
    5. Budget
    6. Value
    7. Trial Solutions

- Trial solutions are a critical element of needs analysis, and can be used to accelerate and clarify the remaining steps of the sales process.

Exercises

- List the things you need to know from a client that relate to your specific product or service before you can write a proposal. Start by brainstorming and then review old proposals to see if there are any elements that you missed. Make this into a list, and keep it with you as you work with clients. There is nothing wrong with referring to it in a meeting, near the end of the meeting, to make sure you did not miss anything.

- On a separate list, identify the kinds of pain your company can solve and what questions you can ask your client to help them discover that pain. The best way to secure a sale is to lead the prospective client through a series of questions that allow them to see what is wrong. If you start by knowing where you want the conversation to end, and ask the questions that get you there, then the prospect will not only have ownership of identifying the pain, but will see you as a partner capable of solving it.

- Bring points one and two of this exercise section together by reverse engineering the conversation, and develop a system for starting and managing the needs analysis conversation in a way that you get to the right answer as a matter of course. Your experience with the client may be different than exactly how you mapped it out, but having the map and trying to stay with it will greatly improve your chances of keeping the conversation focused on getting you to a place from which you can close a deal or at least set up the right solution.

- Make a list of the company, product, or industry specific things you need to learn as a part of the needs analysis stage. Add this to the first list you made, and make sure you cover everything before you suggest some kind of a solution.

- Make a habit of testing trial solutions during the needs analysis phase, and make note of the ones that relate most directly to the solution of the pain.

- Find the right way to phrase a question that concludes the needs analysis phase.

CHAPTER 7

Process Shortcut #2:
The Professional Close

This chapter describes the second of the two "process shortcuts," the professional close. You may choose to use it exactly as described. I do. It is highly effective and completely within the honest, helpful and high-integrity style I use with my prospects and clients. Whether or not you use it as a closing technique, it has value in clarifying the steps of the sales process that we have described so far. Even if you wait until step 7 to close, using the elements of the professional close along the way will help you close whenever you decide to do so.

Up to this point, we have talked about four out of the seven stages of the sales process. The steps that have been taken so far are the most critical for success. Your ability to finish the process successfully (make the right proposal, successfully answer objections, negotiate, and close the deal) are a direct reflection of the leads you chose, the rapport you established in prospecting and qualification, the extent to which you qualified them, the manner in which you conducted your needs analysis, and the information you learned about the prospect and the pain they may need to solve from the first part of the process.

All that being said, there is no rule that says that you can't take a shortcut. If you have done everything correctly and completely to this point, you can consider moving directly to the close. For almost all selling situations, I suggest using something called "The Inoffensive Close," as described in *Baseline Selling—How to Become a Sales Superstar by Using What You Already Know About the Game of Baseball* by Dave Kurlan. In my training and coaching practice, I modify that close just a bit, and I call it the Professional Close, but the credit for the idea is clearly attributable to Dave Kurlan—thanks, Dave!

Here is how it works:

Step 1

When you think you are done with the needs analysis phase, restate the basic findings that you have uncovered, and ask the prospective client:

"So at this point, do you think that I fully understand the issues that we need to resolve?"

If the prospective client says "no," then probe more until the answer to the question above becomes "yes".

Once the answer becomes "yes," go to step 2.

Step 2

Step 2 *usually* happens after the proposal stage.

When you are ready to present your solution, first remind the prospective client that you covered all of the issues in needs analysis by listing them again, and remind the prospective client that you both agreed that all of the major bases were covered. Allow them to acknowledge this agreement again.

Then, after you have presented your solution, ask:

"So, does the solution I have presented solve the problem within your budget, and in a way that you think my firm can deliver the solution?"

If the answer is "no" to any part of that question, then revisit the proposal. The three distinct pieces of this question are:

1. Do you think that this solution, as described, solves the problem?
2. Do you have the budget to solve the problem as described?
3. Do you think that my company can do the work that solves the problem?

If the answer to all three elements of the question is "yes," or once the answer becomes "yes," then the third question is short.

Step 3

"Great—so when can we get started?"

or

"OK, then how can we proceed from here?"

This sounds quite simple and it is. It is, nonetheless, quite powerful. By using this technique, you encapsulate and summarize the entire process into a quick dialog that confirms the need, the solution, and the close.

Front Loading the Professional Close

Now here is the front loading magic: If you have done a good job with trial solutions in the needs analysis phase as described above, then you actually have a tentative proposal as soon as you are done with needs analysis. You can make sure that this is the case by comparing the bullet points you list to the client as the issues uncovered by the needs analysis to the mental list of trial solutions you have suggested. If you have suggested a trial solution for each, or at least almost all of the issues discovered in the needs analysis, then you can go right to the professional close before you formally present your solution. In other words, your professional close comes after needs analysis, and step 2 of the professional close sounds like this:

"So as we were discussing the issues (in the needs analysis phase), I floated some tentative solutions. Can we review them?

For Issue A, we agreed that approach Z might be effective; for Issue B, we discussed how approach Q would be the best approach; and for Issue C, we decided that we would wait until Issues A and B were done, but then we would reconfigure area X to get the resources to solve the problem.

Generally speaking, does this approach to the solution sound like it will solve the problem within your budget, and in a way that you think my firm can deliver the solution?"

If the client disagrees, then probe until you get agreement. Once you have this tentative agreement, congratulate yourself! You have a just reached agreement on the major pieces of your offer before you took the time to write it, answer a single objection, negotiate any detail, or attempt to close.

The client may not accept this, stall, or randomly start bringing up problems with the plan, but it is better to sort that out now than later. Now, you are still trying to find the solution together. Once you submit the formal proposal, you are negotiating, answering objections, and closing—things that can be hard for some salespeople. Why not close the deal first?

Recognize this: By following this technique, you have put yourself in a position to close early. Failure to close due to objections by the client now means that something would have gone wrong later, after you put the work into formalizing the proposal. The pain and the solutions that have been agreed to by both parties are either real or they are not, and the prospect is either qualified or not. Pushing towards a logical and cooperative agreement now will flesh out problems you would have encountered later, so let's agree that it is better to do it now!

In other words, you are now attempting to close at step four in the seven-step process, and you haven't even written a proposal or made a PowerPoint presentation. You'll probably still have to do those things, but by the time you do, it is a validation of the sale you already made, not a bunch of work that you had to do to try to make a sale.

A colleague once asked me what kind of closing ratio I had on the proposals that I present to my prospective clients. His face dropped when I answered 90+ percent. I then explained to him what I just explained to you and it all made sense to him. The secret "trick" is not writing great proposals, it is writing them AFTER you have already agreed with the prospect on what should be in them. If a proposal is a validation of things you have already agreed on with your client, then by definition they are not a vehicle for debate as much as they are simply the formalization of an agreement that has already been made between you and the client.

The proposal, or "presentation of the solution" as it can more generally be called, is still an important element of the sales process, and most likely you will have to make one before closing the sale, so let's address that part of the process in Chapter 8.

Review of Key Points

Chapter 7
Process Shortcut #2: The Professional Close

- If you have done everything correctly and completely to this point, then you may be able to close the deal now using the professional closing technique.
- The professional closing technique has three steps:
  1. Ask and work toward a "yes" answer to the question: *"At this point, do you think that I fully understand the issues that we need to resolve?"*
  2. Ask and work toward a "yes" answer to the question: *"Does the solution I have presented solve the problem within your budget, and in a way that you think my firm can deliver the solution?"*
  3. If you get a "yes" to the two questions above, then you are ready to suggest moving forward into implementation of the solution.
- Step 2 usually occurs after the solution-proposal phase, unless you do a good job with trial solutions as described in the needs analysis section. In this case, you can use the set of trial solutions as a proxy for the solution, and use the professional close after the conclusion of the needs analysis step.

Exercises
- It is a good idea to mentally map out how you will go through the first four steps, including the use of trial solutions, to set up the professional close at the end of the needs analysis phase.
- Write down the exact words you will use for the three professional close questions. It is important that you are comfortable with the words you use, and that you can ask them in a confident and clear manner.
- Now mentally map forward. How will you write the proposal after you get agreement to the three professional close questions? Is there anything that you did not cover in the earlier stages? Prepare to ask those now. The client may be surprised that you are ready to go,

so help the client feel comfortable by going through a checklist of things you need to get before formalizing the solution. Let them know that you are on top of all of the details—that is why they will buy from you without much resistance. Your advanced preparation will not only help you close the sale earlier than expected, but will help the client feel like this accelerated pace is not a problem. If you show that you are in control, the client will be more at ease.

CHAPTER 8

Sales Process Step #5: Presenting the Solution

Definition of Presentation the Solution (Proposal)

Salespeople present solutions to their clients in many ways. A PowerPoint presentation, a verbal description, or a written proposal are among the most common in professional sales. For the sake of definition, a proposal is simply a scope of work or a product and a price. It can be as simple as a retail clerk holding up a pair of jeans and telling you the price, or a 500-page proposal for the development and construction of a commercial property. If it is a communication to the prospective client about what is being sold and what it will cost, then for our purposes, it is a proposal for a solution.

Some Thoughts About the Presenting the Solution Step in the Process

I took a sales assessment test several years ago. The results made me very angry, mostly because they were so true. One of the findings was that as a salesperson, I was vulnerable to prospects who said: "Let me think it over." In case you are not clear on this, "let me think it over" is an objection, also known as "the stall." It usually comes right after you present your solution.

The way I knew that the assessment finding was true for me, was by reflecting on my behavior. I would get through the needs analysis phase, then tell the client that I would write a proposal based on my findings. This allowed me to leave the meeting without asking any tough questions about price and budget, or trying to pin the client down to a commitment.

I would then go back to my office, write up the best proposal that I could, and send it to them. The next few days or weeks were filled with lots of follow up calls or emails. When I would finally reach the decision maker, I was often told some variation of "we need to think it over." My methodology was very psychologically safe for me, but it was not very effective.

Recognizing this allowed me to fix it. The problem is very common among all kinds of salespeople, so let me share some ideas with you about how to avoid this trap in your own sales career.

Whether or not you used trial solutions, you can go a long way toward success at the end of the needs analysis stage by framing the next step. What does that mean?

At the end of needs analysis, you want to tell the client in general terms, but as specifically as possible, what the scope of your proposed solution would be and what it will cost in general terms. If you are prepared to run back to your office, hide behind your computer, and try to write the world's most persuasive proposal, then you have enough information to at least generally describe the scope of work and a general price to the prospective client before you leave the meeting. Doing so will probably save you enormous time and will dramatically increase your likelihood of success.

You might say something like, *"Well, based on what we talked about, I think that the proposal I'm going to write would include the following five main points (list the points). Does that sound like the right approach?"*

If the client does not agree with your summary, you've saved a lot of time already. Go back, and keep working until you can get agreement about what should be included in your proposal. Once you do, say something like:

"So to do all of that, I estimate a roll out time of X, and a cost of Y. Do you think that makes sense?"

If you get agreement on price, delivery time and other elements, then say:

"OK, so we know what we need to do and how much it will cost. What has to happen on your side to get us to implementation once we send you the formal proposal?"

Guess what—you just closed your proposal before you wrote it!

But wait. What if the answers to the questions are: "No"? Then you are lucky to have asked them—think about it:

What if the client says "no" to your approach? Isn't it better that you learned that now rather than after you took the time to write your proposal? Clarifying now allows you to fix it before you write it, and to get buy-in from the client before you suggest the price.

What if the client says "no" about the timeline and the price? Again, you have the opportunity to fix it, clarify it, modify it, or to decide that it is not possible to do business together. If your most bare bones solution is 10 times the money the prospect can afford, then it is better to agree on that now, rather than after sending and following up on a proposal, going a few more rounds on how to make it work, and so forth. Losing the deal now is better than inevitably losing it later after putting more work into it.

The level of detail you can present as a pre-proposal solution suggestion will vary by situation, but you should try as much as possible as early as possible to be as specific as possible. Your success in the qualification and needs analysis phases are where you will lay the groundwork for success at this point in the sales process. Being thorough now saves everyone a lot of time and trouble, and helps you to move past the hard parts of selling—objections and negotiations—without much to deal with. Did you notice that? We closed before we even got to objections. How's that for an objection handling technique—avoidance!

Remember my 90+ percent proposal close rate answer to my colleague? Then you remember that it was because I don't look at proposals as a part of the sales negotiation. In my mind, where applicable, a proposal should be a written confirmation of what has already been agreed upon. If you never take pen to paper (or finger to keyboard) until you have agreement, then you too will close near the range of 100 percent of your proposals.

Now I realize that in many selling situations this is not possible. If you work with large, institutional clients, and they send out blind tenders or RFP's, then this can be difficult. Or if there is a purchasing manager between you and the real client in the company, you may not be able to get the information you need to take this approach. In those cases, you know what to do, because you are already doing it.

There is nothing specific about how to write your proposal that I can tell you. Every situation is different. The work you do before writing the proposal is where you can make a huge impact on your success, or on saving yourself the time wasted on a proposal that is destined for rejection. If techniques for writing great proposals are what you are after, there are plenty of books on proposal writing that you can consult if you insist on that approach.

However, I ask you to consider this. If you have some clients with whom you can pre-agree on a proposal and some you can't, which is the better client? Can you survive and thrive in your business without the latter? If you can, your time will become much better spent by focusing on those clients you can talk to and work with before writing proposals. If your idea of selling is proposal writing, and your driver of success is the effectiveness with which you write proposals, then your skills are not necessarily what I would call sales skills. They are valuable, but if I am managing an organization, I would have some people doing sales as described in this book, and others writing blind proposals. In my mind, it is just different work.

The bottom line is this: Proposal writing takes time and energy. If at all possible, work hard to make your proposal writing something that happens after the sales negotiation is done. If you can't, recognize that your close rate will be far less than if you can, and consider what that means about your time and energy, and your overall effectiveness as a salesperson. If your organization as a whole is facing this challenge, suggest that sales and "blind" proposal writing are two different functions, and ask your managers to help choose the one that suits you best, and to find other resources for the other.

One last thing—proposals written after they are agreed to can be a lot shorter too. They are simply memorandums of agreement, so there is no need for all of that fancy fluff you used to put in to make them more "sale-able." If you have already sold it, then just make a clean professional document that states what you are going to do, how long it will take, how much the client needs to pay, plus the other details that apply to your situation. No one likes to read a long proposal. What a tremendous amount of time you can save all around!

You Are Ready to Move on From This Step When

You are ready to move on from this stage when the client has your final proposal. Now you either get a signature on the bottom (or the relevant equivalent in your world), or you get objections and negotiations, which we will address in Chapter 9.

Review of Key Points

Chapter 8
Sales Process Step #5: Presenting the Solution

- Proposals that present a sales solution differ widely from industry to industry. For our purposes, a proposal is a communication to the prospective client about what is being offered and what it will cost.
- A final proposal will be more effective if it is the confirmation of an agreement already reached, rather than the first vehicle for communicating your proposed solution.
- If you are prepared to write a proposal at the end of needs analysis, you should be prepared to walk the client through the main points of the proposal in a less formal manner before doing the work of writing or otherwise preparing the final proposal.
- Proposals written after they are already agreed to can be shorter than ones that you feel you need to sell—one that may contain things the client doesn't want.
- Proposals written after they are agreed to are not only easier to close, but are actually already closed before you begin to write.

Exercises
- Develop a script and practice the questions you will ask at the end of the needs analysis phase. Remember, you end the needs analysis phase by confirming that you have all of the information you need to gather.
- Next, develop a script for the questions that refer to the general points to be addressed in a proposal, and a general estimate of time and cost.
- Now develop a script for the follow up question, along the lines of: *"OK, so after I deliver the proposal, what needs to happen to bring the project to fruition?"*

- If this kind of a direct approach is not possible for some or all of your business, consider the value of the business that it is not possible for. Either make plans to concentrate on business that can be closed in this way (to save you the time and trouble of chasing blind RFP's) or consider strategies to help your RFP's become less blind, such as asking questions, or getting into the process early enough to help frame the RFP in your favor.

CHAPTER 9

Sales Process Step #6: Objections and Negotiations

Definition of Objections and Negotiations

There are a lot of potential ways to define objections and negotiations (e.g., individually or together). For our purposes, let's group them together and apply the most useful approach at the expense of a perhaps more linguistically correct one.

From this perspective, objections and negotiation attempts are best thought of as questions that must be addressed after the proposal has been presented.

Prospecting objections were discussed in Chapter 3 and are addressed in even more detail in Appendix B of this book. This chapter will focus on objections and negotiation attempts that occur with respect to the sales we are trying to make, not with respect to a meeting that we are trying to set.

Some Thoughts About the Objections and Negotiations Step in the Process

Objection Avoidance

You may think that objections and negotiations are a "necessary evil" in your sales process, but that does not have to be the case. If we answer all of the questions, cover all of the issues, and make sure that all of the relevant information is fleshed out during the qualification and needs analysis stage, then what is left to discuss after the proposal is written?

We have defined objections and negotiations as questions that come AFTER the proposal is given. These tend to seem a bit confrontational and threatening since an offer has been put on the table, and now that offer needs to be defended.

If, on the other hand, questions come up during needs analysis, they are just questions, and don't seem threatening at all. The difference is your thoroughness and professionalism during needs analysis and qualification. If you flesh everything out, and confirm it before the proposal, there is nothing left to do but write up what was agreed to and sign it. No objections. No negotiations.

Here is an example. Let's say that you propose a trial budget in the needs analysis phase by saying something like, *"Well, what you just described to me will probably cost somewhere in the range of $25,000. Do you think we will be able to find room in your budget for something like that?"* When this is addressed at this stage of the process, and the answer from the client is an emphatic "no!" then you can simply ask *"Well, what kind of budget do you think we will have to work with in order to address these issues (that we have just identified in needs analysis)?"* At this stage, you are simply having a conversation and exploring possibilities.

On the other hand, if you make a formal proposal that includes a price tag of $25,000 and the client objects or attempts to negotiate, the tone can be much more confrontational and much less cooperative. It is best to address the objection before the proposal, when it has not yet matured into a full-blown objection and is something you can work with, rather than something you need to defend. In this respect, we are avoiding objections by addressing them *before they become objections.*

Jedi Mind Tricks

But let's face it, the world is not perfect, and no matter how thorough you are in needs analysis, something usually pops up as an objection after the proposal is presented. I am convinced that some prospective clients view the objection and negotiation phase as a form of sport, and they are just not satisfied making a purchase unless they go through a few rounds of "battle" with the salesperson.

So what should we do?

First of all, start by thinking about objections and negotiation attempts the right way. Some prospective clients will use objections and negotiation tricks as tactics to get a better deal; some just have questions or concerns. It is better to assume the latter, even if the former is true. If you start to battle your client at this stage and make them feel like you are trying to "win", the outcome is probably worse than if you handle the situation in the same non-confrontational, cooperative manner in which you have handled the entire process so far. Here is how to do that:

When an objection comes, or when a negotiation is started by your prospective client, keep this idea FIRMLY in your mind:

"If my offer is fair and offers value, then an objection or an attempt to negotiate is probably based on a lack of information that the prospective client has about my product or service. It is, therefore, incumbent upon me to remedy this lack of understanding, and to try to help the prospective client see the fairness of the price, the value of the offer, or the importance of the item they are questioning so that they too can then see how fair and full of value the offer is."

This may sound naive, or idealistic. It is not. What it is, in fact, is the right mental position for you to take in order to begin the objection and negotiation handling process successfully. If you believe in your product, believe your price is fair, and most importantly, if you truly believe that your prospective client's decision to work with you under the terms outlined and at the price given will add value to their situation, then this is the ONLY professional perspective for you to take when preparing to answer an objection or to enter a negotiation.

The result of taking this approach is that your responses will naturally and seamlessly lead you to explore the objection together with the prospective client, or to engage in a clarification of the things that need to be negotiated. It is a more cooperative approach than antagonistic. Your assumption is that you and your client are on the same side, trying to find a way to make this work. Even if this is not true, due to some ill intent on the part of your client, it will be easier for you to uncover any ulterior motives by exploring the ideas that underlie the objection or negotiation tactic rather than by confronting the issue with some kind of a "frontal attack."

Think Aikido rather than Karate; Tai Chi rather than boxing; grace under pressure rather than an escalation of aggression.

How does this philosophy embody itself? In other words, what should you actually do when you get objections and your prospective client starts into some kind of a negotiation posture? Each situation will be different, but the mindset looks like this:

Start by asking clarification questions—think "Colombo."

- *"So what I'm hearing you say is XYZ, is that right?"*
- *"Let me make sure that I understand your concern here."*
- *"I'm not sure that I understand exactly why that worries you. Can you help me understand how this will impact your firm?"*

Sometimes, if your client hears the objection back because you asked them to restate or clarify it, he or she will realize that it does not make sense. If that doesn't happen, then the act of explaining it back to you in more detail may help them resolve it on their own. If none of those is true, this technique gives you time to consider your possible moves forward.

It can also be helpful to think of objections as your client saying, *"I'm not ready to buy yet, but I'm not sure why, so I'll just say this."* When you force them to confront what they said (as opposed to challenging it), they may see through their own stalling tactic, and move on without too much help from you at all—sometimes, you just need to point them in the right direction.

From time to time, a client actually may bring up a valid point. A concern they've only just realized, or an element of your proposal that won't really work. I can't tell you what to say here. If the concern is real, you can rely on the fact that you have established rapport and trust and you are an expert in your field; then position yourself to work with your client to find a better solution together. Being the expert who is here to help pays off at this point, as you are the partner who is already trying to help fix your client's problem. Sometimes you get to do this, sometimes it is frustrating and/or fruitless. Welcome to the real world! However, even attempts at cooperative problem solving that end in frustration are better than the normal jousting that takes place at this stage as a result of more amateur sales approaches. I know you know that; we've all been there. Try this new way on for size. Lay the right groundwork, and this part is a lot easier.

The Objection Quarantine

What happens if the objection is real and not immediately resolvable, or if the negotiation point is firm and apparently unresolvable? If you have ever run into something like this near what you thought was the end of a long sales process, then you are familiar with the knot in your stomach that comes with the realization that the problem is real, you don't know how to solve it right now, and if you don't, you can't win the deal.

It is easy to let something like this derail a conversation. Most salespeople in this situation will stop selling and run off to solve the problem. Unfortunately, that means they've forgotten something important. What if there are other objections as well? They can become quickly reminded of this probable situation when they come back from their creative problem solving work to find that the objection they just solved or the negotiation point they just got agreement on was not the last one. Back to square one, as they say!

Before you disengage from the sales cycle to solve the immediately unsolvable issue, make sure that you have identified ALL of the possible sticking points. Try saying something like:

"Assuming I can show you that it is just as effective, what would you do then?"

"If this wasn't a problem, then what?"

"And if this wasn't an issue, then what?"

"If you didn't have this concern, then what?"

Either the client says that this is the only outstanding issue, and you can have him agree to move forward—if this one issue is resolved—or you flesh out other issues that you can solve now or add to the *"OK, if we solve these then we're done"* list. Guess what? You just closed the deal, contingent on one or a few specific, pre-agreed upon points. Great work—now go solve that problem (or three) and come back to a closed deal.

While using the quarantine technique, you may find that the issue you are trying to quarantine is only the first of a long list of objections that remain to be resolved. In this case, you need to evaluate with the client whether it makes sense to move forward. You should also reflect on your qualification and needs analysis work to see if there was some work that you could have done there to prevent this problem now.

Either way, the attempt to quarantine saves time. It saves you the time of solving one issue only to come back and find more, it saves time in ensuring that you are dealing with all of the unresolved issues at once, and it saves time in the event that the process of fleshing out the unresolved issues reveals that the effort to resolve them all is impossible, and the deal is destined to fail. Better to find this out before doing a lot more work!

Last Words on Objections and Negotiations

Objections and negotiations are not a problem when you know your position, operate with professionalism and integrity, and keep your head. Most importantly, do the steps before objections and negotiations correctly, and this will be a small part of your job. Close the deal after the qualification, needs analysis, or presentation step, and you can eliminate objections and negotiations altogether. Really!

Some of you are probably feeling like this section hasn't said anything at all about objections handling or negotiating techniques. In a way, that is true, but if this is your immediate reaction, you may be missing the bigger point.

Throughout the process, up to this point, we have stressed the need to be thorough and professional every step of the way. If you have, then you have prospected and qualified well; you have done a thorough needs analysis and received confirmation that it is complete; and you have prepared a proposal based on pre-agreed terms, including price and timing. When you approach the process in this way, then objections and negotiations can really be effectively handled as described in this section.

There is no magic bullet that solves all problems, overcomes all hurdles, answers all objections and wins every negotiation. However, your methodology of detailed, knowledgeable, client-focused professionalism carries into this phase, and allows you to move more gracefully through it than if you had taken a more shortcut-filled approach. If you skipped some steps leading up to objections and negotiations, they will catch up to you here. If that is the style you prefer, then get a book on objection-handling techniques and another one on negotiations. You'll spend more time here than you need to, so brush up on those skills!

You Are Ready to Move on From This Step When

Objections and negotiations are over when both sides agree that all of the elements of the proposal are mutually beneficial. Not much left to do now but formalize the deal and move forward. We call this the close.

Review of Key Points

Chapter 9
Sales Process Step #6: Objections and Negotiations

- The most useful way to think about non-prospecting related objections and negotiations collectively, is as questions about your proposal from your prospective client, that belie a lack of information or understanding on the part of the prospective client.
- Objections and negotiations usually come up in reference to some specific element of your proposed solution, and usually come up after you have presented a solution with an associated price.
- Using the techniques described leading up to this point, it is conceivable that you could close your deal without any specific objections. If they can be addressed before the formal proposal is written, then they are just questions.
- When objections do come up, they are best dealt with starting from the perspective that your offer is good and fair, and you simply need to get your client the information required for them to see that.
- Start answering any objection or attempt to negotiate by confirming your understanding of the issue. Sometimes, a client will retract upon hearing the issue related back to them, or you may have simply misunderstood something.
- If you get an objection or a negotiation point that you can't address immediately, agree to a follow up plan for that objection, and make sure there are no more. This way, when you come back with the information for the immediately non-answerable objection, you will be ready to close, not to face another objection. Secure conditional agreement first.

Exercises
- Think about and write down the objections that have prevented you from closing business in the past. Don't forget to include things like, *"I need to think about it," "We don't have budget for that,"* and *"I'll need to review this with _____."*

- For each objection you listed, ask yourself if there was something you could have done differently at some earlier point in the sales process to prevent the objection from coming up at the end.
- For each objection listed, role play in your mind or with a colleague how that objection could be handled from the perspective that the client just needs to know more about your offer to become as convinced as you are that this is the right approach for them.
- Practice with a colleague responding to your most common post-proposal objections with clarifying questions, such as, *"So what I'm hearing you say is..."* and *"Let me make sure that I understand your concern here...."*
- Practice with colleagues and clients the "quarantine" technique. If you leave a meeting with an objection unanswered, then make sure that it is the last one, and that answering it will result in a sale.

CHAPTER 10
Sales Process Step #7: Closing the Deal

Definition of Closing the Deal

Closing the deal is simply the formal conclusion of the business development process. It is the specific instance when both the prospective client and the salesperson agree in concrete terms that they will do business together.

Some Thoughts About the Closing the Deal Step in the Process

I'd like to say that I don't believe in closing techniques. When I first started selling, people talked about closing techniques like they were tricks. They had special names and specific little things you were supposed to do or say at some given time. It made sales seem like something cheesy—not like what I wanted to do for a living. Some of these included:

The Ben Franklin Close

This close uses the story that, when Benjamin Franklin had a big decision to make, he would take a piece of paper and draw a vertical line down the middle. On one side of the list, he would write down the positive things about making the decision and in the other column, he would write the negative things about making the decision. To use this close, the salesperson tells the prospect about this decision-making method and suggests that it is used for the prospective client's current decision. The salesperson does the writing and prompts the prospective client to list all of the positive things about buying. The salesperson usually does not prompt negative reasons from the client, so it becomes a case of two people working on the positives; one on the negatives. At the end, there are usually more positives, so the salesperson can declare that it would be good to move forward with the purchase.

The Assumptive Close

In this close, you make an assumption about closing the deal. My favorite example is from my wife, or rather from me, as told by my wife. (I don't remember it happening this way, but I'm the husband, so let's face it, the way I remember it doesn't matter.)

One night, at the end of a late night date in the early stages of our budding romance, I pulled into the parking area of her apartment complex and, according to her, asked, *"So where is the best place for me to park the car overnight?"*

My question assumed that I, or at least my car, would be staying the night, which was not something that had been previously discussed. A classic assumptive close. The effectiveness of this specific example is outside of the scope of this book!

The Alternative Choice Close

In this close, you give the prospective client two choices, both of which are an agreement to buy. For example, *"So do you want this car in red or blue?"* *"Would you like to pay cash or charge it to your credit card?"* or *"Would you like to take it with you, or should we deliver it to your home?"*

These all feel like tricks to me and, as a sales professional, I don't see my job as tricking someone into making a purchase. So I use other methods.

I would also like to say that there is no need to close. When properly executed, the sales process seamlessly leads to a close. I believe this is true, with one caveat. The salesperson *does* need to say or do *something* to close, because if the salesperson doesn't, there is a probability that *no one will*— and that is not a good outcome.

So how can we close in a way that is professional, easy, and consistent with the way that we have moved through the sales process so far?

If we look at the way that I have described the sales process, it should be fairly obvious that everything has been done in order to lead to the close.

- We qualified our prospects before getting into needs analysis to make sure that if we did our jobs as salespeople well, then they would indeed be able and likely to buy from us.

- If appropriate, we attempted to close the deal right after qualification with a mini-contract.

- We did our needs analysis with plenty of business issues alongside the necessary product specific questions, and we sprinkled in plenty of trial proposals along the way.

- We attempted to close the deal right after the needs analysis phase, at least to the extent that we reached agreement on what needed to be in the proposal—including price—before we wrote the proposal.

- We wrote our proposal to meet the agreements that had already been made, so as to avoid the need to deal with objections and negotiations after the proposal (since they had already been addressed before the proposal was even written).

- In the event that objections and negotiations did come up, we approached them as miscommunications to be clarified. Since our perspective is that we are experts, we covered everything, our proposal has value, and any questions, issues or other concerns at this point MUST be a function of the information in the client's head not matching the information in our head. In this case, our job is simply to clarify that discrepancy.

So by the time we get to the closing time, the time when the last of the objections have been discussed and the negotiations that may have come up feel resolved, the **BIG CLOSE** itself should be pretty simple and straight-forward, something like:

"Great, then let's get started!"

"OK—sounds like we have a plan."

"What kind of administrative requirements do we have to complete before we get started with the work?"

Now a lot of these may sound like assumptive closes, so ruefully described above, but they are not. The difference is that the agreement to work to-gether is not an assumption. We have been clear, honest, value-oriented, and customer-need focused throughout the process. We have communicated with the client about all of the issues, the value, the price, the implementation—everything—up to this point. There is no stone unturned; nothing to do but move ahead in a win-win, mutually beneficial cooperation. No tricks. No assumptions.

Face it. A client won't get this far with you unless they have a need, and if you do the first five steps properly, the rest (objections, negotiations, and closing—so often the bane of poor performing salespeople) just happens, as long as you guide it on the downhill ride it takes to get to "done."

I don't like what have traditionally been called "closing techniques," but I don't think that the sale will close without some proactive nudge from the salesperson. That said, IF the close is properly set up, the conclusion for both parties to move forward should be obvious to both sides, and the salesperson should just be able to point that out, and get the deal.

For those of you who feel like this section should be full of tricks to over-come a client who won't allow himself to be closed, you are missing the point. Most sales efforts do not fail at the closing of the deal; rather, they fail during the execution of the process. If you get past all of the other stages and can't close, you missed something along the way, and no clever closing trick will help you.

You Are Ready to Move on From This Step When

Your deal is closed with a handshake, contract, cash transfer, high five, victory dance, or whatever is appropriate for your business. The main idea is that this marks the end of the sales process and the start of the delivery phase of your cooperation with your client. Once you have satisfied the requirements of the finance department of your organization and also that of the client, and you are ready to talk about delivering your product or service in a specific way—no longer in theory or in a hypothetical way—then you are ready to call yourself done with the close—in a successful way.

Review of Key Points

Chapter 10
Sales Process Step #7: Closing The Deal

- Closing the deal is simply the specific instance when both the prospective client and the salesperson agree that they will do business together under the terms agreed to by both parties.
- Traditional closing techniques like the assumptive close or the Ben Franklin close don't often work, and will be seen by your best prospective clients as amateurish attempts to manipulate them.
- The need to close exists, but needs to be seen in the context of the process we have developed so far.
- If the steps in the process are properly executed, then closing is as simple as confirming the agreements and shared observations that you and your client have made together throughout the sales process to this point.

Exercises

- Stop using closing techniques. Period.
- Review the sales process as described in this book up to this point, and see how this properly executed, thorough, and proactive process leads to a logical conclusion, which is a close. If you believe this to be true, consider what closing question(s) best suit(s) your style.

CHAPTER 11

Developing Your Process-Based Sales Activity Plan

Now we have a sales process. If we use it the right way, it will make our selling efforts more efficient and more effective. This chapter will describe how to take what you have read in this book and turn it into a personalized sales process that will make you more efficient and effective in your selling activities:

First, do ALL of the exercises from Chapters 2 through 10. This includes choosing your prospecting methods and making a plan of action for each one. (Appendix A will help you here.) This will be the core of your selling system. Include the work from Appendix B, the section on the "SCORE call," or Sales Communication Request. This will be the core of your prospecting efforts. Appendix C will help you prepare for objections in the prospecting phase. Each of these Appendices is like a mini-workshop to help you develop effectiveness at getting people into the process. You can't work prospects through the process until they are in the process. Get good at this part, and the rest will come much more easily.

The exercises in Chapters 2 through 11 and the work in Appendices A through C will help you prepare for execution of the entire sales process. Do that work now, and then come back to this page.

Second, assign and track some metrics to your prospecting efforts. The word "metrics" freaks out most salespeople and puts most managers into some kind of a numerically-induced trance. Salespeople think of metrics as information that they need to generate for management—the generation of which is in conflict with their sales efforts. Managers tend to think of metrics in an overly complex way; for example,*"How will I incorporate these metrics into our new enterprise software management system?"*

Don't.

For our purposes here, this does not need to be complicated. Set up some numeric goals for your prospecting efforts that include completion dates and specific activity levels, then track as follows using the tracking systems below.

Don't forget that existing clients are also potential prospects. Existing clients should always have a place in your prospecting plan, so include that method from Appendix A alongside the others that make sense for you. Whatever system you or your company uses to track existing clients, be sure to track them as potential prospects for future business as well.

To generate the most useful metrics for each prospecting method you use, track your efforts with a table or spread sheet that includes the elements listed below. Please be sure to visit our website at www.davidmasover.com/download-forms for editable, downloadable sample templates.

Tracking Lead Sources

The first thing you should track is the effectiveness of your lead sources. No matter which ones you choose, set up a spreadsheet or a table that captures:

- the type of lead source
- the number of people you attempted to contact (i.e., how many people came to the seminar, etc.)
- the people you can successfully move along in the process (i.e., the ones you can call for a meeting)

This will help you to determine the most efficient and effective lead sources for setting up the SCORE call. Visit the website www.davidmasover.com/download-forms for an editable, downloadable sample of the lead source tracking form.

Tracking Prospecting Efforts

Track the effectiveness of your SCORE calls using a table that includes the elements below:

- date;
- times (focus and batch your calls so that you can see how much time it takes to generate each meeting);
- source of contact information (lead source, prospecting method to set up the call);
- number of dials;
- number of conversations;
- number of meetings scheduled.

This will help you to learn how effective each source of names is relative to the others, and how much time it takes to get a meeting, and so forth. It can be more elaborate than the table you will find on the website, but it doesn't need to be. Visit the website www.davidmasover.com/download-forms for an editable, downloadable sample of the prospecting effort tracking form.

NOTE: If you want to get a feeling for how much time it takes to generate meetings, be sure to batch your efforts as described in the sections on prospecting and leads, and note the start time and stop time of each effort on a separate tracking sheet or sheets.

In other words, if you start making calls at 9:00, write 9:00 on the top of a blank, new prospecting tracking sheet. Do nothing but call until the time you decide to stop. Let's say that it is 10:30. Write 10:30 at the top of your prospecting tracking sheet. If your method were cold calling, for example, you would count the number of dials, the number of conversations, and the number of meetings. Doing this will allow you to get a feel for the ratios, and the amount of time it will take you to set a certain number of meetings. If you use different lead sources, or different SCORE scripts, you can compare the effectiveness using similar simple ratios.

For example, if your company exhibited at a trade show and you got leads from the show, track them separately from leads that your company generated through advertising. This will allow you to see and demonstrate to your company which leads are more effective for you. In the case of the trade show, you might list the number of leads collected, the number you reached after the show, the number that agreed to take some pre-defined next step in the sales cycle, and so on.

Remember, these first two tracking systems are only to track the lead sources and the prospecting methods and efforts. Also keep in mind that there are only two kinds of prospecting efforts—making a request for meeting call *without* advance preparation and making a request for meeting call *with* advance preparation. These first two tracking systems are ONLY for those calls designed and executed in order to request the sales conversation meeting.

Tracking Prospecting Opportunities

Once the prospecting effort is a success (i.e., you have a meeting), you should use a third system to see how you move each opportunity through the sales process. The two tracking systems above will help you to track your effectiveness at getting opportunities INTO the sales process. This next opportunity tracking system will help you to see how you move opportunities THROUGH the sales process.

Most companies have something like this; it is generally called a pipeline. Most companies I have worked with don't necessarily capture the right information in their pipeline. It is not often evident from the data that is captured how and how quickly a prospect is moved through the sales process, which is critical for you to understand. This will allow you to see how many prospects make it through the pipeline to a close and for those that don't, where exactly the problems seem to happen, which allows you to consider how to fix that part of the sales process or lead generation source or method.

Once you have a meeting or an agreement to talk with a prospect, move them onto an opportunity tracking system that includes the items listed below. If the pipeline that your company uses does not have enough data for you to track progress through the sales process we have defined, either suggest adding these elements or make your own tracking system. This is not complicated or time consuming, and it will provide you with very valuable information about your efforts and opportunities for improvement.

Opportunity Tracking Elements
- lead source
- prospecting method used
- opportunity name (person, company, or both)
- date opportunity identified (when the SCORE call was a success)
- date of first meeting
- date qualification completed
- date needs analysis completed
- date solution/proposal presented
- objections and negotiation issues resolution dates
- date closed
- result (win or lose)

Visit the website www.davidmasover.com/download-forms for an editable, downloadable sample of the opportunity tracking form.

You can add more items if you determine them to be important, such as identifying key issues, timelines, or decision influencers as a part of the prospecting or qualification process, but essentially, you want to know how long it took to get from one step to the next. Leave the details of what it takes to get from one step to another in another document. If it is clear what it takes to be qualified, we only need to track how long it took from the time the name was generated, the meeting was set, and the first meeting was held until the time that the qualification, as defined elsewhere, was completed. If the elements of qualification are the same, there is no need for it to be a part of the tracking. It was either done, as clearly defined elsewhere, or not, and by when. The same goes for the transitions between other stages as well.

Using these simple tracking systems and some pretty basic calculations and/or spreadsheet functions, you should be able to track and evaluate the following things, which are key to understanding how effective you are at moving each opportunity into and through the sales process.

Are you meeting your prospecting commitments?

Using the prospecting effort tracking system, compare the number of prospecting efforts versus the goals and commitments you made about prospecting as a result of the work you did in Appendix A. If you are not meeting your commitments, why not? Many salespeople rationalize that they are too busy with existing clients to prospect. This may be OK from time to time, but not as an ongoing practice. Whatever your excuse might be, be honest with yourself. Were expectations too high or execution too unfocused? Part of the value of the process is helping you to see where you are not fulfilling the tasks needed to be more successful. If this is really true, then how are you prospecting for new business with existing clients? Track that, and be proactive with your client base to maximize value and to connect to as many potential buyers as possible at the client company. Cheat here, and you only cheat yourself.

Are your prospecting methods generating a sufficient number of meetings for the time/money/efforts/hassles they require?

You may find over time that some prospecting methods work better than others. As long as you don't put all of your eggs into one basket, such as choosing a method that limits the range of companies you may get as prospects (e.g., not enough industry diversification, wrong or incomplete revenue targets, methods that do not reach decision makers in correct way or at all), then go with what works. Use your tracking system to help you decide what that is.

Are you converting enough opportunities identified into meetings?

This is a simple ratio that you can track over time, against yourself in different time periods, against your peers, or use to compare different lead sources and prospecting methods. If you are struggling here, consider the source of the leads, the method of prospecting and the tactics of your prospecting efforts. As you make changes, let them be executed for a while so that you can see if the change has a positive or a negative impact on your results over a reasonable period of time.

Are the meetings resulting in enough qualifications?

If not, are you meeting with the right people? Are the qualification criteria correct? What needs to change to improve this? If we are to divide the sales process in half, this is the key moment in the first half. The second half is where the money is, and you should not go there until you qualify. What can be improved?

Are you able to complete needs analysis?

If not, why not? Was this a function of the person you are talking to (e.g., improper qualification or poor lead criteria), or is it a function of the way you conduct needs analysis?

How long after the needs analysis did you submit the proposal?

Is this a reasonable amount of time? How much time are you investing in the preparation of proposals? Did you confirm key elements of the proposal before you wrote it?

What kind of objections did you get?

Pay special attention here. Try to learn how you could address these objections earlier in the process next time. As previously mentioned, I like to prospect using seminars, and I design the seminars to answer all of the objections I can anticipate. Questions you ask and trial solutions you propose in needs analysis is another area in which you can preemptively address objections and negotiation points before they actually come up.

What is your closing ratio?

How many meetings with prospects turn into business? How many qualified prospects become customers? How many proposals do you write relative to the number you close? Evaluate these ratios to see where you can improve, or where improvements have happened. If you use a new source of leads, is there an impact on your closing ratio? This is good information to have, and may not be as apparent as you think until you track it.

This kind of tracking is not time intensive or complicated. For prospecting efforts, you make a mark in a box with each dial of the phone, each conversation, and each meeting set—total time per effort, about six seconds. Calculating the ratios won't take you much longer.

Opportunity tracking will take you a little more time, since you need to type in the name of the prospecting method and the opportunity (15 seconds) and a date in each box for each successive step in the process when that step happens (as a normal part of your sales work—five seconds times six steps), and finally the outcome (15 seconds). One minute of data entry for each prospective opportunity. May you be blessed with a shortage of time to do this work. Calculating the ratios is a spreadsheet function that you will set up once, and the information you get will help you identify areas in your sales process that need work.

The big bang-for-the-buck, however, is not commensurate with the minimal effort. Once the system is designed, tracking takes very little time, but the time you spend analyzing the results of the tracking will be the most important time of your week. Since we are reviewing simple ratios over time in a pre-defined process, this is an analysis that will take minutes, not hours. Review your numbers with your manager if you can, or by yourself. Learn your own weaknesses. Get a book, get a coach, go to a training, fix it, give yourself a raise and take some time off.

If you want to excel in your work, make your efforts more effective and also more efficient. What has been described so far in this book, and specifically in this section is a clear, fast, and easy way to do it. I know of no other that is as powerful. I hope that I have convinced you to try.

Now that You Have a Working System, How to Manage Time and Clients

I have seen IT more times than I wish to count (IT being the word "it" with emphasis, not an abbreviation for Information Technology). First in my own career, then from my colleagues, then from the salespeople I manage, and from almost all of the salespeople, sales managers, and sales executives with whom I have ever worked as a consultant.

What is "IT"? It is the problem that occurs when in the normal course of business, one accumulates too many names. How can there be too many names? Is this not a sales book? Names are the front of the funnel—so what is the problem?

There are at least three problems:

Problem #1: Having too many names to manage.

This can take the form of a stack of business cards toppled over on your desk or in a database that is too full of names to be managed effectively.

Problem #2: Not knowing what to do within your scheduling system with a prospective client with whom you just finished a communication.

OK, you have just hung up the phone or ended a meeting. It felt positive, but what really happened? And what is supposed to happen next? You should probably schedule some kind of a follow-up contact, but what? When? It seems silly when you just read it like this, but think about it—you know it probably happens to you several times a week.

Problem #3: Not knowing what to do with the name of a person with whom you just made contact.

This is that person you met at the networking event or trade show, or at the playground. You exchanged cards. Now what? Yeah, it probably goes into the stack or the database and becomes part of problem number 1 or 2 described above.

These are all manifestations of the same problem, and—as the core message of this book would lead you to believe—one that a well-defined sales process can help you to manage.

Believe it or not, this won't be a CRM discussion. Why? Ask the next business process expert you meet how well a CRM works without a business process to support it. Software and systems are worthless, unless the right business process is behind them. If you know what the steps are in your process, and how to get from each to the next, then you know what to do with discreet pieces of data (like names and conversations) because they all of a sudden have context.

If, on the other hand, you don't have that process and that context, the CRM won't help you. It is just a more complicated software-based stack, or a specific graphical interface for a database to put names into, but not in any kind of a meaningful way.

So how does our process help? If you look at a contact name, or a communication event and try to decide what to do with it, it will be easier if you have a framework against which to compare the situation. If you do, then you can say, *"OK, the process looks like this, and this person is at point B in the process, how can we get to point C?"* It is just that simple. If you don't have the framework, it is hard to know what to do with the name, and paralysis sets in. Over time, this kind of paralysis manifests itself as a big stack of unfiled business cards, a database full of unclassified records, and an overall ineffectiveness in dealing with each and all of the names you manage as a part of the efforts you make to sell your product or service.

In other words, if you get a business card, it is a lead. You should try to set a meeting to qualify the prospect. If you qualify them, then they are in your process; if not, then you can consider them some kind of a non-sales contact in your contact management system.

In another situation, when you hang up the phone with a client, you can decide where they are in the process. If you are in the middle of an active sale, what stage are they at and what comes next? If they are not in the middle of an active sale, when is the best time to schedule a contact to see if you can get a new sales process started? Over time, you will train your mind to think in terms of the process, and you won't end the conversation until you have confirmed the next step in the process.

Only when you can put an item into the appropriate context can you think about the item in relation to other items, and thus evaluate it accordingly, effectively, and efficiently—meaning quickly and correctly.

The Bottom Line of Selling

When I was in college, I realized that the best professors were not the ones with lots of fancy jargon related to their field of specialty, or very complex theories that none of the students could understand. The best professors were the ones that could illustrate quantum physics using an analogy about an apple and a pencil, or a nuclear power plant litigation case using the analogy of an oil change shop. In striving toward that level of clarity, allow me this:

This book and the appendixes that follow have over fifty thousand words, but if I had to boil the essence of sales and the sales process down to three words, they are these:

What happens next?

Everything you do in sales should end with some agreement between you and the client about what you will do next.

The sales process, as defined above, is the guide (i.e., what *should* be next).

If you did the work to clearly define what is required to happen in each step of the sales process, and what needs to happen before you move to the next step, then answering the question "what's next" becomes easy. Each communication you finish, each name you see, each contact in your database can be thought of in terms of where they fit into the sales process. If we do that, and then ask the "what's next" question, what to do next with all of our contacts and with all of our communications becomes clear.

To apply this to your total database, business card collection, and so forth, you will need to do the work of going through each name, and for some of you that will be a big job. However, it is a much bigger job to go through the names if you don't know what to do with each one. If you DO know what to do with each one, then going through them is just work.

For a job like this, I suggest salami.

Have you ever heard of the salami technique? The idea is this: No one believes that they can eat a whole salami in one sitting, but if the salami is cut into slices as you watch a sporting match on TV, it is amazing how often a person can get through the entire salami before the end of the match.

In that spirit, deal with 10 or 20 or 50 names a day—schedule time to go through a set number of names like you would schedule a meeting, and plug them into your system using the process criteria you created using the appropriate chapters in this book and the "what's next" question as a guide. Eventually, you'll be done with the salami, and will be on top of your database as well.

Database Maintenance

First, a lot of the people in your database will be people who have been collecting proverbial dust, so you'll have to decide what to do about them without the benefit of any recent contact. What should you do? Change that. What a great prospecting opportunity—make that number 22 on our list. If you call everyone you ever put into your database just to "check in" and see what's going on since the very long time ago that you last talked, you'll accomplish a lot.

- You'll know where to put them in your follow up system, if you ask *them* when you should follow up.
- You'll remind them that you exist. Whenever I did this, a lot of people said that nothing was going on at the time I called, but a few of them usually called back with a project later that month. I had been registered in their minds. My call was like an advertisement, and the next time they had a need that related to my product or service, they thought of me.
- You'll also get the opportunity to thin out your database.

Sometimes, and regularly, you need to purge your database.

Just like pruning the trees in your garden every spring, you need to get rid of the "dead wood" in your databases. You may not necessarily need to delete them, but you should consider classifying names in your database in different ways. Differentiating between those who have the potential to buy from you or not is obvious. If someone does not have the potential to buy from you, then you should not be trying to get him/her into your sales process.

The harder ones to consider are those who potentially COULD be in your sales process, but for some reason just are not buying from you. You'll need to make your own rules, but over time, you need to either get them to buy from you, or stop spending time on these folks—maybe give them to marketing to be added to the newsletter mailing list, or make a quarterly newsletter yourself and send it out. This way, you'll have a lot of people see your name, but those who don't seem inclined to buy don't get more time than it takes to push the "send" button (even better if it is automated). If they do decide to buy sometime in the future, they will remember you from the newsletters, maybe even buy from you, and then you can take them off of the low time commitment program and classify them as a client. If they continue to never buy from you, then your time with them is minimal at most.

Let me illustrate this with an example. I am the co-founder of an Internet company that still thrives as of the publication date of this book almost 10 years after the dot-com bubble of 2001 and (currently, in 2009) in the middle of the second US economic meltdown of its history. The company does a great job of getting people to register on the website, and uses the registrations to feed the salespeople a steady diet of qualified leads.

The problem was that over the course of a few months, not to mention a few years, the salespeople would get VERY bloated databases. I took the senior sales team through a program where we identified an average of two thousand names in the database assigned to each person. After some analysis, we found that on average,

- about 10 to 15 percent of the 2000 contacts had bought something at some time (200-300);
- about 80 percent of those 200-300 contacts that had EVER made a purchase, made one within the last 12 months (160-240).

When we arranged this group of recent purchasers in rank order from highest sales volume to lowest sales volume and added up the sales total cumulatively from top to bottom, we found that the top 30 percent of this list accounted for 80 percent of the sales volume for each salesperson in the prior 12 months. These numbers are approximations, but on average, we were down from 2000 contacts in each database to about 48 to 72 contacts per salesperson worth paying a lot of attention to (30 percent of the 80 percent of the 10 to 15 percent).

All of a sudden, the salespeople did not feel so overwhelmed by the number of names in their databases. They had classified each name according to the value in sales dollars over the last year, pulled out a few hot prospects that had not had enough time to gestate, and started using their newfound free time to prospect for more people to fit into the top producing part of their newly lean-and-mean database.

Guess what? The old 80/20 rule works. It is not precise, but it is a good general rule. How can you apply it to your bloated list of names you are calling a client list? Should you be spending the same amount of time with each person in your database, or are there some different classes of clients and prospects for you to use?

When a time-intensive special request comes in from a name in your database, it should matter if they are a big part of that 80 percent of your revenue, or if they are someone from a big company that calls every once in a while for a special project, then never buys. Do they all deserve the same amount of time? Do some of them justify more qualification before that investment of time? You bet—discriminate accordingly.

You need to prune from time to time. You need to know who is putting commission in your pockets and who is wasting your time. Clear out the dead wood to make room for some new growth. The work can be tedious, but once you do it, maintaining is not so hard. You'll be glad you did. Now go clean your room, and give yourself a raise!

Bringing It All Together

Your job as a salesperson is pretty simple. Get people engaged in the sales process, and get some of them successfully to the end of that process (a successful close).

To make the magic really happen here, you just need to go through the work of making each step of the process concrete and detailed. This will give you the context within which to evaluate each prospective opportunity in terms of the three key things you need to know:

1. Are they worth sales effort?
2. Where are they now in the sales process?
3. What needs to happen next to move them definitely either forward or out of your process?

If you can remember this level of simplicity in your job, and apply the discipline of your sales process to your efforts, your work will be more efficient and effective than you ever imagined.

Would you like to be a top producer in your firm and still be home in time to have dinner with your spouse and kids? Or to make it to the gym? Or out to dinner with a friend? You can. You have just been given the map.

Review of Key Points

Chapter 11
Developing Your Process-Based Sales Activity Plan

- To develop your own process-based activity plan, start by choosing your prospecting methods. (See Appendix A for a mini-workshop to help you with this.)
- Assign metrics to your prospecting efforts; track them; and stick to them.
- Assign metrics to your opportunities and track them.
- Analyze where and why opportunities fall out of your process to help you find areas for potential improvement.
- Develop systems for allocating time to the right clients and not too much time to clients who are not buying enough from you. Your total sales revenue and your average client value will increase if you do this on a regular basis.
- Develop systems for tracking names and opportunities within the context of your sales process.
- The bottom line of selling is ending each sales communication event by answering the question "what's next?" The answer can be, and often should be, "nothing," but moving through the sales process effectively is about answering that question in context.
- Thin out your database on an ongoing basis.

Exercises
- Do all of the exercises from Chapters 2 through 10, if you have not already done so.
- Assign metrics to your prospecting efforts and create tracking mechanisms.
- Create a tracking system for your opportunities.
- Set up a meeting with yourself for an hour a week or more if you can, to go through all of the names in your current database, and to contact and reclassify all of them to allow you to focus on only the strongest prospective clients.

CONCLUSION

Warren Buffet has an expression about investing that applies to sales, in a slightly modified form:

"Sales is simple, but not easy."

Very little in this book is new. The information here is not highly innovative. Nothing in this book is complicated. It just works!

Success happens when you execute with forethought and discipline. This book has just shown you how to do that.

Your goal here may or may not be to become a sales superstar, although you might get there. Your goal should be effective, efficient execution. Doing that with a lot of focus and intensity might get you to super-stardom. Doing it 40-hours-a-week will probably get you into the top third of your sales organization, and still allow you to have a life.

Front load your process. Do the early parts of the process with great care, and you can minimize the parts of selling that most people don't like, and don't do well.

Follow a well-developed process, practice with discipline, and get help along the way. This is a proven path to sales success.

If each salesperson operates this way, everyone wins. The salesperson who is a professional; the human being who wants a life outside of sales; the family of the salesperson; the company the salesperson works for; and the customer who buys what the salesperson sells.

Let's not forget the customer. His or her interests are also served—by an expert who is there to help, executing with discipline, and making sure that no one is wasting their time.

APPENDIX A
PROSPECTING METHODS IN DETAIL

In this appendix, I will describe in more detail each of the 21 prospecting methods mentioned in the prospecting section of the sales process. In order to create an individual sales activity plan, you should consider each prospecting method to determine if it is suitable for your specific situation.

Each individual method has many details, strategies, and possibilities associated with it. It is beyond the scope of this book to cover each one in great detail. Several books have been written on each prospecting method. If you find a method that works for you, then you should study that method in detail to ensure that you are executing it with the maximum levels of efficiency and effectiveness.

Once you have identified the appropriate prospecting methods, you will need to assign some numbers and metrics to each one—how many, when, how often, and so on. (Please see Chapter 11 for more details on the metrics you should track for each prospecting method you choose.)

Developing these methods, assigning metrics and holding yourself accountable to the completion of these efforts according to your schedule are the most important things you can do to advance your sales career. The rest of the process is certainly important, but unless you do this first part—getting people INTO the sales process—the other parts never get a chance to be done. If there is nothing IN the sales process, there is nothing to get THROUGH the sales process.

So let us look at our 21 methods. If you have a prospecting method that is not mentioned here, please visit my website www.davidmasover.com/contact-us, and let me know about it. If it is indeed new and different, I will post it on the website and add it to future editions of this book, credited to you.

Proactive Prospecting Methods

This first group of prospecting methods is called "proactive" because you have to do something proactive and direct in order to get engaged with the prospect. These are the methods over which you have the most control.

1. Cold Calling

As mentioned earlier in the book, cold calling is unlike every other prospecting method listed here. In all of the other prospecting methods, the goal is to create a reason for making the call. In the cold call, you initiate the call with no prior contact or context for a reason, so developing the right reason and crafting the right way to say it are critical. (See Appendix B below for more on this.)

One of the key elements in Appendix B is the scripting of your SCORE call. This is especially important with a cold call. Your success will be based in large part on the first impression that you make on the recipient of the call. What you say will be important (the reason), but how you say it can make or break the call. Speaking with relaxed authority will take you a long way toward success. Scripting the first 30 seconds of the call will help a lot! You will probably be nervous, so be sure to follow that advice and the other guidelines in Appendix B in order to enhance your success.

There is not a lot to say specifically about cold calling that is not mentioned in Appendix B, but one thing is important. The time of your call may make a bigger difference here than the timing of calls that have a pre-established reason. Here are a few schools of thought to consider:

Call before or after working hours

This takes into account the fact that during working hours, a gatekeeper might answer the phone, but early in the morning or very late in the afternoon, when the secretary has gone home, the boss or other more senior person that you are trying to reach may pick up the phone directly. If this feels right to you, try it.

Call before their day has happened to them

I have always found the most success with cold calls comes when calling before 10:30 a.m. My theory is that people come to the office with some degree of optimism about their chances of having a productive day. However, the more the day goes on, the less optimistic they become. Distractions, new projects, unexpected meetings, or crises all come up to detract them from their plans. Your unexpected call in the middle of this will be less welcome than it would be if it came early in the morning when there was still hope for a productive day.

Either way, time your calls, practice your script, focus your effort, and just start dialing. Track your results over time using the tracking sheet available at www.davidmasover.com/download-forms, and decide for yourself if this can work well for you. Executed properly, cold calling can be very effective and efficient. I won't promise that it is fun, but I'm pretty sure that no one has ever died from trying it. You will need to give this a real effort before making your decision. See my numbers in the Leads chapter for validation of this point. Making five cold calls and giving up is not proof that cold calls don't work. You will need to do better than that.

2. Company Generated Leads

If you are lucky, your company does something to generate leads. Perhaps advertising, attending trade shows, or encouraging registrations on a website. If this is the case, then the way the lead was generated becomes the reason for the call. Do the exercise in Appendix B, and for the reason, simply use the way the lead was generated. For example:

"Hi, Mr. Jones, This is David Masover from ABC Company. I'm calling because you registered on our website, and I wanted to introduce myself to you. I am your personal account manager, so if you have any questions or need any help, I am here to support your web experience to make sure that you get all the help that you may need from our service. Is there anything that I can help you with now?"

3. Networking

By networking, I mean using the people you know to generate business. Networking events and groups are a separate method and will be discussed below.

When you are attempting to use friends, family, and other existing contacts to generate business, it is best to be short, direct, simple, and un-repetitive in your efforts. Something like:

"Hi John…by the way, I'm trying to develop more business for my company and I'm hoping you can help. The target prospect for me is X, Y, and Z. Do you know of anyone like that who you can refer me to?"

It is important that you make the target clear. Let your friends know exactly who you are looking for in a lead. Give this some thought before you ask, so you can ask in a clear, but concise way. If they come up with a name, be sure to get contact details and get permission to use the name of your friend in the introduction; or better still, ask them to make the introduction for you.

By un-repetitive, I mean don't keep bothering them. Ask once, and then stop. You will alienate your friends if you ask them for business leads every time you see them. If your company makes some kind of a promotion for referrals, or if you have some new offering, then ask again. Otherwise, tap this network once, and move on. Don't lose your friends over this!

4. Trade Associations
Working with trade associations as a form of prospecting can take two forms. The first is the most obvious, and least useful. This is the idea of joining your own trade association, or in other words, the trade association associated with your own products or services. This is the least useful for prospecting purposes because the association is probably not full of prospects for you, but rather, competition. It is possible that the association is broad enough that both competitors and prospects are members; if this is the case, then becoming VERY active might differentiate you to the prospects from among the competitors in the group. In this way, it could be useful as a prospecting venue.

A more useful approach is to join the trade associations of industries that are likely to be your prospects. For example, if you sell promotional items, you may want to join a trade association related to trade shows, industrial safety, or travel and hospitality. These three industries are heavy users of promotional items. You can justify your presence there by letting people know that, as a professional, you are interested in knowing what issues concern your clients in their field of experience, so that you can better provide the kind of service they need from your specific perspective.

Toward the end of making this justification seem legitimate, give some thought to your reason for being there in a way that will make sense to those in the industry who might ask. Your objective for this mini-speech is to help them understand why you are there, and to help them see that you are someone who may provide them with a service that they may need. If you can accomplish the latter, then this becomes a great prospecting venue. Those to whom you give the speech will be inclined to believe that you are a service provider they need, and who is professional enough to spend time understanding their issues. A good way to start a relationship, don't you think? They will too.

5. Formal Networking Groups

Formal networking groups exist in most cities and in many forms. Some are organized in districts within a city, and allow only one person from each specific profession to join a given chapter. For example, each chapter may have a dentist, a lawyer, an accountant, an insurance agent, a real estate agent, and so forth. If a group already has a dentist, then another dentist can't join.

The idea is that the group meets every once in a while to exchange leads. Some of the people who need lawyers may also need accountants, and so on. If you are going to join a group like this, make sure that the group has policies about exchanging leads, not just intentions. It is too easy for everyone to show up looking for leads, but for no one to bring any. If everyone in the group is open to ideas about how to increase lead exchange and does so, then it may be a good group for you. The "reason for the call" will be a mention of the name of the person who gave you the lead, and the rest is up to you.

Formal networking groups can also take the form of business mixers or networking events that are held from time to time and sponsored by a variety of organizations. These can be inefficient prospecting methods if there is no focus around the kind of prospects who may choose to attend. You will likely spend at least 10 minutes talking with a new person you meet, and chances may not be high that they are a prospect. Even so, you are still talking to them. This may be pleasant, but not necessarily useful or efficient with respect to prospecting.

One strategy for maximizing the prospecting effectiveness of business mixers is to volunteer to give a short presentation to kick off the event. This will allow the organizers to advertise your subject matter and attract interested prospects while giving you the chance to let everyone know what you may be able do to help them. Think of this as a mini-seminar, and read the section below on seminars to maximize the effectiveness. After your presentation, people will approach you, and know just what to talk about.

6 . Referrals and Introductions

Your clients are the best sources of referrals. Period. But you need to ask. Most salespeople don't. Don't be one of those. If you find the right time, then it is easy. Some books have been written that tell you to start talking about referrals from the first minute you meet someone all of the way through the end. If that feels right to you, then go for it! I have found that there are a couple of key times when asking for referrals are the most welcomed by the clients and the most fruitful:

1. Just after you complete a project or a significant piece of a project, during that smiling, handshaking, group self-congratulatory moment, it is a great time to say something like, *"Listen, this has been a big success; do you know of any other people or businesses who might benefit from something like this?"*

2. After they decide not to do business with you—and you've put a lot of time into trying to make something happen, but you did not get the deal because the deal will not move forward— it is a good time to ask. You will leverage sympathy here. Say something like, *"I'm sorry that this did not work out. Do you know of anyone else that might benefit from this kind of service?"* Don't try this if your competitor got the business, only if you lost the business because the business simply will not happen.

3. At the end of your first meeting—in the first meeting, you had a chance to explain what you do in more detail—take the opportunity to ask, *"Well, now that you know a bit more about what*

we do, is there anyone you know of that might benefit from learning more about our services?"

These are all examples of requests for referrals. To make them more powerful, turn them into introductions.

To do this, simply follow up an agreement from the client to make a referral with something like:

"Thank you. I really appreciate you giving me those names. In my experience, the people I am referred to are usually a lot more open to meeting me if they get a call first from someone they know. Would you mind calling them and letting them know that I will be contacting them?"

The worst thing that happens is that they say "no," and you are still richer for having the referral. If they say "yes," then your introduction is even stronger.

7. Electronic Networking Groups

Electronic networking groups are things like LinkedIn (www.linkedin.com), Xing (www.xing.com), and others. I differentiate these from social networking groups like Facebook (www.facebook.com) because sites like LinkedIn and Xing are designed for business users to connect with each other for the purpose of doing business. There are consultants, books, strategies, and theories about using social networking sites for business. If this is of interest to you, there are plenty of resources you can consult, so I will not try to address those here.

Rather, let's focus on the sites that are made for this kind of business networking, although not always used for that.

If you have a profile page on LinkedIn or Xing, chances are you don't do much with it. I have been active on both—more so in the past than now—and I have noticed that very few people are proactive with them. Most people also tell me that they do not work. Well, I suppose if you put up a profile and no one finds you, you can say that it does not work, but there are other possibilities.

When I first moved to Hungary, I needed to generate business among people who spoke English. I turned to LinkedIn and Xing (then called OpenBC) and used them like electronic cold calls. The default language of these sites was English at the time, so I immediately knew that anyone I contacted would be able to communicate with me. Both sites are becoming more international, and other language choices are now available, but the possibility to filter by language is still there. Not true of the cold calling I tried first.

So I wrote a script, searched for specific kinds of companies that I thought might need my services, then sent the exact same email to each one. Out of 20 messages sent, I usually got four or five responses. Of the four or five responses, one or two were positive, and led to a meeting. One out of every three or four meetings turned into business. That meant that if I sent out 10 messages a day, or 50 per week, I could count on generating about one or two pieces of business a week. Since sending out 10 messages took about an hour (I had to find the right recipients first by searching the database), that meant that one hour a day of prospecting got me 50 or so pieces of business a year. Not bad.

I made a discipline of adding as many contacts as possible to my network, as this allowed me exposure to more and more contacts. Over time, I used LinkedIn and Xing less and less, as I had built up a strong non-virtual network of clients and contacts that I could use for referrals and repeat business.

One of the other things that these electronic networks are good for is their special features. LinkedIn for example has a question-and-answer section. If you need some advice, ask a question. If you want to be seen as an expert in your field of expertise, then answer some questions. Do note that one of the LinkedIn categories of questions and answers is called "Using LinkedIn." If you have a question about how to be effective with LinkedIn, you are probably not the first, so look through the questions that have already been asked and answered, or ask your own to help make you more effective with this fast growing and highly useful platform.

On Xing, there are features to organize and promote local events. Make your own networking events and invite who you want. This can work for networking events, seminars, or any other way you can bring people together who might be interested in your product or service. Remember, the goal is to connect with people who you can follow up with to set a meeting. Get creative; these tools can help. Be proactive, and you might generate some business with them. Very effective. Very efficient, if used systematically.

8. Existing Customers

Most salespeople will agree that existing customers are the best source for new business. However, if you dig a little deeper, you quickly realize that many, if not most, of these same salespeople do very little to be proactive about generating new business from this admittedly best source of business. In most cases, salespeople benefit from inertia. The customers are used to buying from them, so hopefully they will keep doing so. There are at least two problems with this approach.

First, if a proactive, deliberate selling effort is not made toward these existing customers, then they are more susceptible to your competition. Much like a lover who misses the intense romantic "honeymoon" period of a mature relationship can be wooed away by a new courtier who smiles, brings flowers, and really appreciates this lonely, neglected soul, so may your client be intrigued by the energetic new salesperson trying to woo their business away from you.

The second problem is this: The inertia effect works well for the things that have always been purchased by your existing clients. However, over time, the needs of your clients may change, as will your product offerings. Your clients may open new branches, production lines, or hire more people; your company may introduce new products, new materials, or new technologies. All of these things should be a part of the ongoing conversations you have with your existing clients over time. They will open up opportunities for you to sell more and for your clients to benefit more from their relationship with you. Remember, you don't sell things to your clients only to make your commission; you sell things to your clients because they need your products and services to help them solve problems in their lives or in their businesses. Keep the lines of communication open and the lines of commerce follow naturally.

How should you do this? Easy. Got a calendar? Got a client list? Match them up. The timing will feel different in each business, culture, and industry, but each month, each quarter, or at least a few times a year, make contact with each of your clients (assuming you have purged your database). Ask what's new since you last talked and tell them about the new developments in your company. It can be as formal as a presentation, or just a stop by for coffee. It is amazing what you can notice just by stopping by. Perhaps a new building is going up, or a hiring campaign is under way. It's hard to know this if you don't check in now and again.

Remember the section earlier in the book on database management? Here is where the "what's next" part comes into play. After you stop in for coffee, or whatever, ask when you should plan to check back. If they give a date, ask what will be happening then and why you should check in, this will give you a reason to call when that time comes. Put this contact in your calendar and forget about them until their name comes up—they are covered. If they don't give a date, then suggest you'll check back in a few months or if something interesting comes up, then schedule it and do so. You will keep the relationship alive, keep yourself in the front of their mind, keep on top of changes in the account, and act as a "scarecrow" for prospective competitors.

One more positive thing happens when you systematize your follow-up schedule for existing clients, and this one is for you.

So much time and energy can be wasted worrying about what we forgot to do. Be disciplined about how you check in and schedule the next check-in with each existing client, then forget about them, knowing that they are managed by your system. You will keep on top of it all, and worry about less in the process. Try it—beats the heck out of just keeping a stack of business cards on your desk and worrying which one is being swept away by your competition this week.

9. Former Customers

Former customers are a lot like existing customers; the only real difference is how much time has passed since the last sale was made. Former customers should be considered as a special category when performing the database maintenance described in Chapter 11. At one time, sometime in the past, they had already made it through the entire sales process, including the part where they made a commitment and bought something. This is indeed significant.

The fact that it has not happened in a long time scares many salespeople away. They start applying the same kind of creativity as our lonely guy in the bar staring longingly at the pretty girl, but not daring to approach her. Our salesperson comes up with all kinds of reasons that the former customer stopped buying:

- Maybe they found a better supplier.
- Maybe we did something to offend them.
- Maybe they went out of business.
- Maybe there is a new buyer who is really mean.
- Etc.

Now it is possible that some, or even all of these things may be true, but so what? The hard fact is this: right now, these are names in your database doing nothing but taking up space and possibly haunting you with some kind of latent anxiety. Want to fix that? Call them.

The SCORE call is very clear. It goes something like this:

"Hi. It has been an awfully long time since we heard from you. Are you still using the XYZ's that we once supplied you?" (if yes), "Oh good, well we've made some changes in the way we do things since we last met, would it make sense for me to stop by for a few minutes next week to show you what's new on our end?"

If that doesn't feel right, then you can try this:

"Hi. I don't think we have been in touch with you since we modified our pricing / specifications / service contract / product offering (etc.). Can I come by next week to show you what we've changed since the last time we met?"

If they say "no", you have the opportunity to find out why they are not doing business with you anymore, and you can cross them off of your list of potential prospects. If they say "yes," then you are into the sales process. This is a no-lose situation. The loss happens when these people are ignored, as is so often the case—don't. There is no upside there. Engage, decide what's next, and schedule accordingly. You either get someone in your pipeline or you make room in your system for someone new in your pipeline. Remember, your job in sales is to get people into your sales process and then get them through. Do one or the other, not nothing, and you are making progress.

Message-based Prospecting Methods

Message-based prospecting methods only work if you have something to say that will interest your prospects. For some of these methods, you only need one interesting thing to say; for others, you need an ongoing stream. For example, you only need to give a seminar once, but if you commit to writing a newsletter every quarter or to writing a blog that you update every day or a few times a week, you need to be sure that you have an ongoing supply of useful information.

Professions in fields such as insurance, law, real estate, and the like, are some obvious examples of industries where practitioners are often exposed to updated information that may be useful for existing and prospective clients. Other not-so-obvious industries also have rich, new nuggets of information that may be worth talking about. Don't take things you know about your business for granted. Remember, relative to your prospective clients, you are an expert in your industry simply because you spend more time paying attention to changes in your field than your clients do. Keep them updated in newsletters, blogs, and seminars, and they will come to see you as the expert that you are. If you use the transmission of information to your best advantage, you can help clients identify needs and overcome objections even before speaking with them directly. Let's look at some of these message-based prospecting methods in detail.

10. Seminars (presenting)
Presenting seminars is one of my personal favorite methods of generating new business. The funny thing is this: I am not a big fan of standing up in front of a group and giving a lengthy speech and/or PowerPoint presentation.

Is this hypocrisy? Not at all. To understand how it is not hypocritical, you need to separate the act of delivering a seminar from the usage of a seminar as a prospecting method.

People tell me that I am good at presenting seminars. I am relaxed; I structure seminars in a way that they are easy to follow; and I add enough funny slides, jokes, and stories along the way to keep the presentation entertaining. I suppose that is nice—it certainly beats the alternative. What I find funny is when people ask me immediately after the seminar, *"So, was it successful?"* In the context of reaching the prospecting goals, there is just no way to know that yet. For my purposes, delivering a good presentation is not the goal of a seminar. It is a prospecting method; as such, the goal is to set up a SCORE call and a meeting that follows that is closable. Those goals are the reason I like using a seminar as a prospecting method. Let me explain:

I like to reverse engineer my prospecting methods, and a seminar is a great way to do that. Let's do it together now:

- Perfect end result: A signed contract for sales consulting services.
- Interim step to the signed contract: Closing a mini-contract for diagnosis.
- Step before that (sometimes): Overcoming objections to spending money to solve the problems.
- Requirement before suggesting mini-contract: Currently unanswerable questions about the status of the sales organization.
- Step that leads to unanswerable questions: Identification of sales issues.
- Opportunity to identify sales issues: A meeting after the seminar.
- Element to get people to seminar: Title for seminar compelling for prospects.
- Effective seminar title: Match up likely client sales issues with solutions that I can provide.

In other words, if I work this process in reverse order, all I need to do is:

A. Create a title for my seminar that is compelling for my target audience because it highlights (and filters for) issues faced by companies that I can help. Something like:

"How to maximize revenue from your sales organization"

A title like this is sure to attract people who have responsibility for a sales organization, and the desire to increase revenue for that organization.

B. Make sure that the bullet points in the middle of the list above (identifying sales issues, currently unanswerable questions and potential objections) blend together as the content of the seminar. The seminar content should be designed to address these issues in such a way that interesting topics are discussed, but only in general terms. This way the clients know that, while I can speak effectively to their issues at the seminar, it can be done best in a personal meeting.

In the case of the example above, seminar content might include:

- The best methods for identifying sales issues (the need for diagnosis).
- The high cost of poor performing salespeople (justification for spending the money).
- The most common unanswered questions within a typical sales organization (to help attendees see similar needs in their own organizations).
- The most useful case histories to show how these methods helped other clients (justification for the meeting after the seminar).

The phone call that follows the seminar and asks for the meeting may sound something like this:

"Hi <name>, I wanted to thank you for coming to the seminar; I hope that it was useful for you. You know, in a seminar, we can only discuss things in a general way.

Do you think it might make sense for us to meet in your office to discuss how some of the ideas we touched on in the seminar might apply specifically to the situation in your organization?"

Once in a meeting, it is obvious that we are there to discuss sales issues as they affect the sales organization of the prospective client, so it is easy to get into that conversation.

Those issues can then be turned into to questions that we don't have enough information to answer until we do a mini-contract diagnosis (which of course leads to more business because of all of the problems we find).

The only point left on our list then is the typical objections that are likely to come up in your post-seminar sales conversation.

Before you create your first seminar, you can probably guess what the objections will be in the meeting that follows. After you do a seminar and the meetings that follow once or twice, you will know almost all of the objections that will ever come up at this stage of the process. Now here is the great part: *you can answer them in your seminar before they are asked in your follow-up meeting.*

I have found that when I sit face-to-face with a prospective client and we have a conversation, they seem to sense that I am a good salesperson. The things I say in response to their questions are designed to address their concerns specifically; however, if I say those same things in a prepared format, in front of a group, they hold more authority. I am not a psychologist, so I'm not going to speculate about why that is, even though I have my own theories, but I can tell you this from my experience.

There is a big difference between answering an objection for the first time in a meeting with a client, and answering that same objections by saying something like, *"As you may remember me describing in the seminar...,"* then answering the objection. The fact that you addressed the issue in public, unprompted, and proactively gives the objection response the kind of weight that you just can't generate with a seemingly spontaneous response.

I love seminars as a prospecting method. They allow me to map out the entire sales process before the attendees of the seminar even take their chairs. After that, going through the process of following up for meetings, qualifying, digging for needs and closing a mini-contract is practically automatic.

It will, of course, be different for you and your industry, but if you take this right approach—that the seminar is the first step in a multi-step process that leads to the closing of a deal—you will be successful.

Most people who give seminars focus only on giving a great presentation to show the audience how smart they are, and hope that the attendees will recognize this and call them for business. Do better than that. The medium lends itself to it, if you take the time to construct it the right way. If you do, the payoff can be huge, and quite frankly, easier to execute than most prospecting methods you will ever try.

You will notice this the minute you sit down for your post seminar follow-up meeting. You are looked at as an expert. Continue to play the role of expert that you started by speaking at the seminar, and watch the business practically close itself.

11. Conferences (presenting)

Presenting at conferences is almost the same as presenting a seminar, with a few key caveats. First, you need to get invited. Second, you may need to conform your comments to some central theme of the conference. Third, you may not be as free to control the content so as to allow you to manipulate and direct it toward your sales efforts. Finally, you may not know all of the attendees or be able to control the capture of their contact information, which may limit your ability to follow up afterwards.

Even with all of these limitations, presenting at a conference can be a big benefit for you. Your personal exposure will be magnified, and the fact that you were invited makes your prestige higher, as perceived by the group.

You can still accomplish many of the same things in this kind of speech as you would at a seminar, such as identifying key issues of your prospective clients, anticipating and answering objections, and laying the groundwork for any potential meetings you might have by pre-addressing issues.

Where you may need to be more creative is capturing names for follow-up. One way to accomplish this is to offer some additional information beyond the content of your presentation. For example, write a short white paper going into detail about a specific issue that will ONLY be of concern to people from whom you could close business. During your speech, ask people to bring you a business card or an email address so that you can send this to them after the show. It is entirely reasonable that you would not have time to go into all of the details during the conference speech, so offer this as an add-on, and you build a list of people with whom you can follow up afterward.

(NOTE: Don't make the mistake of giving your email address on a slide and waiting for people to contact you. Get their contact information, so that you can be the one who makes sure the contact is made.)

Whatever you do, don't just make your speech about showing off how smart you are. Be smart. Think about how you can use this to generate the SCORE call after you are done, and how you can set up the meeting that follows for maximum success. This way you will not only be looking smart, you will be selling smart as well.

One bonus from presenting at a prestigious conference (or at a seminar of some kind) is the business it can help you generate from existing clients and new contacts you meet. If you send out notices to all of your existing clients to let them know about your upcoming presentation, you will remind them that you exist, point out that you are an in-demand thinker in your industry, and may even prompt them to contact you for a lingering problem they need to solve.

Similarly, when you meet new prospects, you can tell them that one way they can learn more about your product or service offering is to come and listen to your presentation at the conference or seminar. Even if they do not attend, knowing that you are presenting is one more piece of information for them that will help to position you as a good potential resource for them.

12. Trade Shows (exhibiting)

Trade shows are a great way to generate leads for follow-up to get people into your sales process pipeline. Accordingly, it is very unfortunate how many ways people find to miss this opportunity, and more unfortunate still that the baby (trade show prospecting) gets thrown out with the bath water, and trade shows come to be seen as a bad prospecting source not because they are, but because of how they are used. Let's first look at a bad example.

The first time that I went to a trade show as an exhibitor was at the Jacob Javits Convention Center in New York. If you don't know this venue, let me just tell you, it is very, very big! I came prepared with a terrific giveaway item that I was sure that everyone would want. I was right and my in-the-booth shtick quickly morphed into a short pitch to all who passed by:

"I'll trade you this deluxe trade show badge holder for a business card!"

It was tremendously successful. My boss was beaming at me working so hard in his booth. All seemed well.

The problem was, I got back from the show with 1500 business cards, and I had no idea which ones were worth a follow-up. I muscled through a few hundred, but no more. The show was, in effect, wasted. Certainly some of the people passing by our booth were interested in what we had, but we had not even asked for, let alone captured that information.

Contrast that with a trade show I exhibited at in Germany with a Polish company that made very complex printed T-shirts. I had some experience in T-shirt printing, but my experience was limited to a few single colors printed on each shirt, or at most a blending of the four basic colors called four-color process. This Polish company, on the other hand, was doing some highly sophisticated stuff. Typically, they printed shirts on what was called a 12-head machine, which meant that each t-shirt was hit 12 times with either an ink, or a chemical to dry or cure an ink, or some other amazing process. Their clients included some of the top retail brands in the world, and their work was stunning.

In the middle of the booth, the Polish company set up one of these 12-head printing machines, and spent three days at the booth printing an award-winning design on red shirts, and giving them out to prospective clients. The booth experience was much different from the one in New York. In this booth in Germany, a lot of people came up to watch the machine in action. It turned out that a lot of them were not prospects at all, just curious about the big machine. Some of them sold competing machines, and some of them were direct competitors of the exhibiting company. But the approach we used made all of the difference in the world:

We asked a qualifying question.

A qualifying question, as you can imagine, is a question that qualifies the person you are asking to see if they are indeed a prospect for you. In this case, we asked something like:

"So can you imagine using this kind of print technology to support your branding message?"

We got a lot of "no" answers to that question, which was great—lots of people with whom we did not need to waste time. However, those who answered "yes" were people with a real need, and a real reason to follow up. Our goal was to find a few dozen very qualified prospects from among the tens of thousands of people at the show, and set up a plan to follow up with them after the show in pursuit of business. The machine got them into the booth, and the qualifying question filtered out the ones with whom we wanted to spend extra time—a good use of the trade show.

Like most everything in life, and most certainly everything in this book, success came from thinking about what we wanted—meetings with people who could use what we had, to further their own business goals, then setting up a situation to make that happen.

Stephen R. Covey in his book, *The 7 Habits of Highly Effective People*, talks about the value of beginning with the end in mind, and that truth applies here as well. Define the goal, then work it backwards to determine what you can do as you execute this and each of the prospecting methods to make it happen most effectively.

There is one other thing to keep in mind about trade shows. It is hard to know which of the people passing by are your best prospects, especially if you are in the middle of a long conversation with someone who came into your booth, and you just can't stop talking to them. There is a great method for reminding yourself not to do this. (I can't recall when I learned about it, if you do know the source, please let me know at www.davidmasover. com/contact-us. I will add it to the website, to the next edition of the book and, if you'd like, I will credit you with reminding me as well.)

The trick is to be Q.U.I.C.K. Most trade shows last only a short time, and it is easy to meet an interesting person and spend a lot of time with them in your booth. What you will notice if this happens to you is that lots of other people walk by, not bothering to talk to you because you are so thoroughly engaged with your chatting buddy. What you don't know is if one of the people walking by is THE person you came here to meet, and you just lost your chance. So be Q.U.I.C.K.! What does that mean:

Q: Qualify - Ask some kind of a quick qualification question before moving forward.

U: Understand the basic need that your solution can fix—not a lot of detail
   here—not yet, not now. Save this for later.

I: Identify some kind of a solution in general terms that you think is worth
   discussing in more detail after the show.

C: Confirm a follow up plan. Let them know when you will call, what you will
   send, or when you can plan to take some kind of next step together.

K: KICK THEM OUT OF YOUR BOOTH!

You did your job here. You set up the SCORE call. You won't do more at the show itself unless it is a selling show, and fewer and fewer are, so move on. Get more ammunition for the front end of your sales process, and go home with a few dozen hot follow-ups, not the 1500 bulky leads I took back from my first big show. Then watch your boss smile as you work them through the process, and close business from them.

(NOTE: Some people may consider attending trade shows a good way to generate business (by walking the floor and soliciting business from exhibitors in their booths). This practice tends to be discouraged by show management in most cases, and many exhibitors will be offended if you are blatantly searching for business as a visitor to the show. The exhibitors spent a lot of money to be there to generate business, and it is easy to look like a cheap freeloader if you attempt to generate business from the exhibitors. These unwritten rules are a little more flexible if you are an exhibitor and you approach selected other exhibitors, but it is worth exercising some caution and using some judgment if this is a direction you are considering.)

13. Writing Articles

When my wife and I first came to Hungary in 2004, no one in the country had heard of life coaching. Those who were told about it were convinced that it would never work in Hungary, due to some perceived intrinsic elements of the culture and the mindset of the Hungarian people. This was a bit of a problem, since my wife had given up her former career as an attorney and dedicated herself to life coaching through an 18-month training program and some initial success as a practitioner in San Francisco before we moved across the ocean.

So what did she do? She made calls to the publisher of every major newspaper and magazine to tell them about this revolutionary self-development method she had imported from the United States. Many of them ignored her, but a few did not, and so began my wife's career in Hungary as a life coach, through the writing of articles.

What is important to remember is that the job of the media is to sell advertising. They do so by filling their magazines and newspapers with content that they think will be new, different, exciting, and interesting to their readers. Your job is to find some angle on your work that is interesting to a group of readers of a magazine in such a way that you position yourself as an expert.

Now my wife learned some tough lessons here. Editors can take great liberty in editing your work, and the final result may not be stated in the way you had meant it. You see this dynamic all of the time on the television news when sound bites are tossed around, and the speaker claims that the small sound bite was taken out of context.

My wife also learned that the magazine will not always support the efforts of their readers to track down the author. This can be overcome by making sure that your name is highly "Google-able" (another easy to research subject that is outside of the scope of this book), or that you can somehow work into the article a mention of your website or blog to help readers find you. Many editors will let you write a small paragraph at the end describing yourself, so be sure to include an email address here, or say something controversial or inquisitive within the article, and invite comments to an email address in your article.

If you have some expertise or some interesting things to say related to your work, then trying to get articles written can really boost others' perception of you in your market. Treat it like any other prospecting method. Schedule an hour a month to developing topics and another hour to trying to contact editors. You might strike gold.

One nice thing about print articles is that they stick around. My wife frequently gets clients from an article she wrote years ago, because the magazine stayed around the dentists' offices, beauty parlors, or wherever. Her online articles continue to be found by people doing web searches for "life coach in Hungary." She works a lot less at prospecting than most people I know, and yet the prospects keep rolling in. She dug a good, deep well, and she just keeps drinking.

14. Newsletters
Writing newsletters is a lot like writing articles, except that you don't need to find an editor, and you need to write with some consistency. What you do need, however, is a recipient list. This is not as hard as it may seem. If you know you will be sending a newsletter each month or each quarter, then every email address you find can be added to the list. Failing that, you can buy or rent lists, or create an opt-in campaign.

(NOTE: Use a newsletter service to make sure that you comply with all spam laws, especially the "unsubscribe" features. If you send these out on your own, you could face some liability issues and associated penalties, which may be quite high. Outsource this for both the ease of administration, and the freedom from worrying about keeping up with the ever-changing laws. There are dozens, if not hundreds, of reputable services to choose from and, with a small bit of work, I am sure you can find one you like.)

One of the really nice things about the newsletter is that you can use this as the least time consuming part of your client communication. As you prune your database as described in Chapter 11, assign some people to the "newsletter only" category. This way, they take effectively zero time, but you still maintain a presence with them.

Be sure that your newsletter has information that will make people think about how they can use your service. For example, if you sell insurance, write about case histories of how extra insurance services not used by most of your clients really helped someone who just faced a crisis situation. Or if you sell exercise services, equipment, or supplements, write about a success story in which you and/or your clients were involved. Some industries even publish stock newsletters and allow you to add your own name and logo.

If possible and/or feasible, don't be shy about adding coupons, special offers, or suggestions for input. Remember, this is a way to get people into the sales process. For many recipients, you can even add a personalized note (if possible) or you can follow up the newsletter with a personal phone call to a particular client to suggest that they read a certain article that you thought they might enjoy.

The idea here is to get people engaged and into the sales process. If something in the newsletter allows you to follow up with a SCORE call, then it has really hit the mark for you.

15. Getting Quoted in the Media
You can benefit greatly by being among the list of people called upon in the media for quotes as they pertain to specific matters in which you are an expert. Your expertise will be valuable if it is appealing to large numbers of people, but also if it is highly specialized. If you are such an expert, then you and your company can benefit greatly by having you quoted in the media with respect to issues and articles that are in the sphere of your domain of expertise.

But what about a more humble occupation like a real estate agent, an insurance broker, or a gardener? Don't sell yourself short. Each of those areas, and whatever area you specialize in, has an audience of people that need to get things done (like an assessment of a home, an estimate of appropriate insurance coverage, or an evaluation of the best fertilizer to use with gardenias). NEVER forget our sales definition—you are an expert in your field who helps people solve problems—and NEVER forget that the function of the media is to sell advertisements by attracting people to the content their forum. It is a match made in heaven; you just need to connect the dots.

There is no formal magic here. If you are an expert, just let the media know. Call your local paper or the publications associated with your trade. Let them know that you would be happy to comment on any article in the range of your expertise, and ask if the person you are talking to is the right person to file away this information. If so, then ask them to get onto your newsletter list.

There are online services that match experts to journalists across the globe for just this reason. Depending on how far you want to cast your prospecting net, the more local approach may feel more right to you—at least as a starting point.

It can be a long way from being mentioned in the paper to getting a phone call for business, but maybe that is not the right way to think about it. What would happen if every time you were mentioned in the newspaper (in a positive way), you cut out the article and added it to a scrap book, or linked the article to your website, blog, Facebook page or to the signature of your e-mail? Over time, you would have a very strong third-party set of references as to your expertise. When it came time for a prospective client to consider using your services, the decision might be just that much easier if they knew how well regarded you are in the media.

This is not a short road to lots of clients, but as the road goes along from year to year, it can become a much more lucrative road for you to travel.

16. Blogs (including community-based forums)

Creating and maintaining a blog is a great way to keep in touch with people who may or may not be your direct prospects, but who are people that are interested in the kinds of things in which your prospects will be interested. The rules and etiquette about how to commercialize, monetize, advertise, and prospect within your blog are fuzzy at best. It seems that the line of "appropriate" online behavior can be crossed rather easily with significant negative results. If you are new to blogging, some of the best advice I have ever heard about getting started is to read blogs for a while, then start to participate in a few. Once you find your "voice," consider starting your own blog, but only after you realize why you are doing it, and what kind of a time commitment it will take to maintain it.

The problem with a blog is that you need to have something to say once or several times a week, and you need to be prepared to respond to feedback you might get based on what you post. However, if you do have something to say, you say it well, often, and you get people to read and interact with your blog, then it can be a great way to initiate specific sales communications and to establish your expertise in your field.

There is a concept called "thought leadership" that should be at least somewhat self-explanatory, and may make sense for your business. If it is important that your clients see you as a thought leader in your field, then a blog is a great place to demonstrate this. Your goal will not be to get prospects out of the blog directly, but rather to let people know you have some solid, original ideas about your subject, and as such, should be trusted with their specific issues.

Blogs, social networks, and many of the so called "Web 2.0" venues are ever-changing landscapes, simultaneously ripe with opportunity, and fraught with unforeseeable traps that are easy for a novice to step into. Accordingly, step carefully, read a lot, get some help, define your strategy before getting started, and hope for the best. Please do share your success stories with the group by sending them to me at www.davidmasover.com/contact-us. While you're there on my site, check out my blog and feel free to add your comments.

Passive Prospecting Methods

Passive prospecting methods are so named because you, the salesperson, are probably not directly involved in organizing them or executing them. In small companies or one-person firms, where one or a few people do everything, the salespeople may be a bit more involved in these kinds of activities, but let's approach this as if the salesperson is not directly involved in these methods.

The point here is that something happens and prospective clients are exposed to the company. Perhaps some formal mechanism is used to capture leads, or perhaps leads come in without some formal capture method. Either way, our sales process starts the same way—there is a SCORE call, and the event that makes up the passive prospecting method becomes the reason for the call.

If you are a commission-based salesperson, or your company is not normally doing these kinds of activities, I would suggest that you do not focus your efforts here first. Since these methods are passive by nature, they don't allow as much direct control, and results may be sporadic in the short run. Longer-term involvement usually pays off here, and may be good for organizations that are looking for multiple methods of lead generation, and any enhancement helps to feed a large appetite for leads. For a single salesperson, however, this is just gravy. The meat of the meal should come from some of the more active approaches described above.

Nonetheless, these can be valuable, so let's explore them for just a few moments.

17. Advertisements

Advertisements are among the most obvious of the passive methods—put up a billboard, place an ad in the newspaper, or even hand out flyers or tuck them into the windshields of cars. Where I live, in Hungary, this is allowed even in the mailboxes of private homes. I often see flyers that have no call to action other than a phone number. Some people even drop off a business card. It is sad to think that people expect results from such untargeted actions.

If you are going to use advertisements, then try to accomplish at least three things as a result:

First, request a specific response:
Your advertisement should say something like "call now to receive," or "first fifty callers will get," or "limited time offer." This will encourage those who are interested to take action now, rather than to "file" it for later use.

Second, make sure that the response is only interesting to prospects:

If you offer a free car, then you will attract anyone who is interested in a free car. If you sell cars, this might be OK, but not if you sell gardening services. Offer something in your ad that will only be interesting to people who may be your prospects. You will receive a smaller number of responses, but those who do respond will be more likely to buy your product or service.

Third, identify the advertisement that led to the response:

It is important for you to learn which messages, which marketing methods, and which demographics work best for your advertising. If you run the exact same advertisement with the exact same offer in three newspapers, how will you know which worked best? Use a separate email address or phone number, promotion code, prize, or anything in each ad so that you can see which gave you the most results for the money you spent. Maybe the one that cost you the least amount of money gave you 50 percent more leads than the more expensive ad. Set yourself up to track your response rates, and you can be increasingly efficient as you go out to market your products and services in the future.

Remember, this like all of the prospecting methods is made to generate the reason for the call. Don't forget to set up the advertisement in a way that allows you to call the prospect afterward, introduce yourself, and see if there is anything you can do to help so that you can get them into your sales process as a result of your advertising efforts.

18. Community Activity

Community activity can be anything that you or your company is involved in that is related to the community—not necessarily in a business context. For example, perhaps your church group hosts a community festival each year, and you work in the booth that makes funny-shaped balloons for the kids. Or maybe you participate in a walk-a-thon to raise money to cure a disease, or you volunteer with a group of people to paint an orphanage, or the home of an elderly resident in your neighborhood. The point here is that a group of people come together for some event that is totally unrelated to your business.

So how is this a prospecting method? Well, it can be to the extent that you will probably meet people during the event, and as a part of the process of introducing yourselves to each other, you will probably mention what kind of work you do. It might help to bring a group from your company, and all wear something with the company logo. (Forgive me, the promotional products salesperson is deeply embedded in my psyche.)

If prospecting is not your objective, it really doesn't matter what you say here. However, if you would like to maximize any possible prospecting potential of the event (i.e., the person you happen to be introducing yourself to is a potential prospect), then you should prepare in advance a concise, clean way of introducing your business that will evoke the right kind of a response from a potential prospect. Let me illustrate with an example.

When I sold promotional products, I found that the term "promotional products" evoked very different pictures in the minds of different people. Some people thought I made happy meal toys for McDonalds, others thought I made items with the logos of sports teams for sale at the stadium during the games. Other people thought I made business cards and brochures. None of those were true, and more importantly, none of them were useful for me as images in the minds of these people if they were to be considered my prospects.

What I wanted them to think about was the items that THEIR company used to put their logo on for trade shows, safety awareness events, company gifts, commemorations, and general marketing purposes. To achieve the right image in their heads, I determined that I needed to talk about my products in a different way.

I would like to give a reference here to the place I heard about the technique I am about to tell you, but I can't remember it. (If you are the originator of this idea, or you remember who is, please contact me at www.davidmasover. com/contact-us and tell me who to credit with this technique in future editions of the book. I'll add something to the website right away.)

The best way to paint a picture in someone's head about what you do is to describe who you HELP and how you HELP them. So in my case, I started saying something like:

"I help companies with usable products, like T-shirts and coffee mugs, that they decorate with their logo or marketing slogan and use to promote events, reward employees, or market their products at trade shows and at corporate events."

This technique can be used at networking events, or anywhere you need to introduce yourself and your company and would like to do so in a way that you qualify prospects. If the person you talk to nods and says, "Oh, that's nice," then you have effectively introduced yourself, which was the objective all along. If, on the other hand, the person you are talking to becomes interested in what you do, then you may have a prospect, and the way you introduced yourself allows you to elaborate and probe for potential needs. You probably won't make a sale here, but you can certainly qualify someone as a prospect that you may want to follow up with in order to set a meeting. You also put an idea in their heads about what you do, that they can relate to other people who may become prospects for you.

If you enjoy participating in these community events, then by all means do so for that reason. Your chances of building a business this way are not as strong as if you do more focused prospecting efforts. However, if you are participating anyway, you might was well have a simple technique like the *"we help people"* method of describing your job to help people understand what you do, and to increase the chances that if they are a prospect, you may even get a meeting with them.

19. Sponsorship

Sponsorships are usually something that happen on the company level. Your company may decide to sponsor a tennis player, a race car, a community sports team, or a community event. If this is the case, then your company will usually get some kind of a venue associated with the sponsorship. This venue can vary from a special tent at the race or the tennis match where you can invite current and prospective clients, or a special event associated with the sports team or community event.

Because these are not meant to be HARD marketing and selling events, your best approach when meeting people in this environment is to use the *"we help people"* form of job description that I described in the "Community Activity" section and see if there is some interest. If there is, then exchange business cards, and plan to follow up later. Then enjoy the event. No one comes to these things to be sold, so lay off. Just enjoy yourself, and make sure you have a chance to set up business later.

One note about exchanging business cards—it is much better for you to get their business card than for them to get yours. Ideally, you will exchange cards, but if you have theirs, then you can take charge of the follow-up communication. Alternatively, you can give your business card to lots of people, and then wait to see who calls. You might indeed get some calls, but what you give up is the possibility to be the driver of the communication. At the very least, program their number into your phone and make the call to set up next steps. If this is about prospecting, then make sure that a SCORE call is the next step, and take responsibility for making it happen.

20. Special Events

Special events are different from community events and sponsorships in that they are usually events that your company may organize. They may be organized as a form of reward for existing clients, like a helicopter ride over the city to showcase a new project followed by a party, or a sailing race like Oracle organizes every year in the San Francisco bay. The thing to remember about special events is that they are primarily for fun. Don't kill the moment by forcing it into a business event. Use it as a chance to get to know people on a level other than business. If a business conversation starts, defer it to a later meeting if you can. The prospective client will appreciate that you are allowing them to enjoy the event, and your efforts to set up a business meeting following the meeting will be welcome due to the fact that you allowed the fun to happen when it was supposed to, without pushing the business agenda at the wrong time.

21. Direct Mail (or email)

Direct mail or email is usually a mass effort going out to a pre-defined list. If it is successful, then the sales department will wind up with a list of people who responded to the mail (electronic or otherwise). The reason for your SCORE call will be simply that—they responded to the mail, and you are following up to see what kind of help you might provide.

Be sure that you know what was in the mail, so that you can anticipate the kinds of questions that may come up. Familiarity with the content will also help you know what kinds of expectations the person who responded to the ad may have. Also find out what type of people the mail was sent to, so that you have some idea who you will most likely be dealing with when you follow up the lead.

Beyond that, this is just another "reason for calling" to insert into the standard SCORE call we will develop in Appendix B, and another way to get people from outside of your sales process into your sales process—as long as they deserve to be there.

APPENDIX B
DEVELOPING THE SALES
COMMUNICATION REQUEST CALL

As mentioned in the prospecting section, there are only two kinds of prospecting efforts. The first is when you request a meeting, usually by phone, without any prior activity designed to "warm up" this call. This kind of a call is often called a cold call. The other kind of prospecting call is exactly the same phone call, only this time you did one of the other 20 things on the list in the prospecting section to "warm up" the call.

In either case, you will need to make the call to ask for the meeting or other communication venue as might apply to your situation. In this book, we have used the term SCORE (Sales Communication Request) call to describe this call. This can be a cold call, a warmed-up cold call, or a call to an existing client about starting a new conversation about a new piece of business. It is, as the name describes, a request for sales communication. It can be used in any context in which initiating communications about sales is your goal.

A few things are critical about this call:

1. You will be more likely to succeed in getting your chance to sell if you:
    a. call the right person;
    b. have the right reason for the call;
    c. speak with confidence; and
    d. focus on getting the opportunity to sell before you start selling.

2. You should script the first 30 seconds, since in most cases, the call is going to have the same first 20 to 30 seconds each time, and you will want to make sure you:
    a. say the right things;
    b. sound confident when you do; and
    c. drive toward a close of this part of the process—agreement to a meeting—with pure precision.

Many salespeople balk when I suggest that they use a script. However, not having a script usually results in a lack of focus and a lot of *"ums"* and *"ahs."* This unfocused, sloppy call is much less fun to do because the uncertainty makes you, as the caller, feel bad, and frankly, makes you less likely to succeed.

So get over yourself and let's develop a script!

The script format below is based on the script development suggestions of Stephan Schiffman in his book *Cold Calling Techniques: That Really Work.* I listened to the audio version of this book in 1995, and have made calls based on his suggestions, taught these kinds of calls, managed the execution of these kinds of calls, and consulted about these kinds of calls ever since. Over time, I added a few twists of my own, but the form is still primarily from Mr. Schiffman. Use this simple guide to develop your own script, and see how easy it becomes to use it for all of your various forms of SCORE calls.

Part 1: Attention

(NOTE: Everyone loves the sound of their own name, so using it will get their attention, while also letting them know that you are calling the right person. If you go through a gatekeeper, ask to whom you will be connected so that you can use their name and not have to go through the awkward task of asking for it halfway through the call or later.)

EXAMPLE: *"Hi ____(name)____,"*

TIME: two seconds

Part 2: Introduction

(NOTE: As soon as you have the attention of the person you are calling, you should answer the first question that comes to their mind: "Who is calling me now?")

EXAMPLE: *"This is ME from MY COMPANY..."*

TIME: four seconds

Part 3: Plug (Optional)

(NOTE: If there is a chance that the person you are calling is not familiar with your company, then develop a "plug," or a short phrase that describes your company in a positive light. This will answer the second question on their mind if they don't know you, which is "What does that company do?" It should come as the second half of the sentence, right after the name of your company.)

EXAMPLE: *"the leading ____"; "one of the ___ in all of ___."*

TIME: four seconds

Part 4: The Reason for the Call

(NOTE: This is the heart of your SCORE call. If the reason is good, you will get the meeting, if not, you won't. It is just that simple.)

If you used one of the 20 ways listed in the prospecting section to warm up the call, then that becomes the reason. In this case, you don't need the plug in part 3. As mentioned in the prospecting section, the main reason you are doing those prospecting activities is to create the reason for this call, right here, so that you can get the meeting. In that case, the reason is easy to develop.

EXAMPLE: *"I am calling because when we met at the conference, you mentioned that you were interested in _____, so I wanted to follow up to see if we could find a time to meet and talk about it in more detail?"*

If you did not warm up the call, then create a reason that assumes they will want what you have to offer. This way, it actually becomes part of the qualification filter. If they say, "no," it may be because they are not qualified, in which case you did not want to meet them anyway.

EXAMPLE: *"The reason I am calling is because your company fits the profile of the kind of companies we help by reducing their office paper consumption by over 50 percent."*

Incorporate a key benefit into the reason for the call. This will help to set up the qualification piece below.

TIME: six seconds

Part 5: Qualification

(NOTE: There is no sense in meeting with someone unless he or she is the right person to make a decision about the product or service benefit that you can offer, so ask here. This also sets up the close.)

EXAMPLE: *"I understand that you are (OR 'Are you...') the person responsible for office waste reduction and paper consumption?"*

TIME: four seconds

Part 6: Validation

(NOTE: Assuming that they said "yes" to the qualification, then you should set up the close. If they said "no" to the qualification, get the name of the right person and ask to be transferred.)

EXAMPLE: *"Oh good—(then you are the right person for me to talk to)"*

TIME: two seconds

Part 7: Set up the close

(NOTE: You will get them to agree to a meeting or other sales conversation if they think that there is a benefit in it for them, so remind them again of the benefit when asking for the meeting. Ask for as much time as you need, but try to promise a short meeting. If the meeting is going well, and you hit the time you promised, but are not done, you can ask permission to continue. The short amount of time suggested at this point will assure the prospect that the time commitment won't be too much, which could be a concern in the back, or front of their mind.)

EXAMPLE: *"Why don't we set up a 20-minute meeting so that I can show you the kinds of savings we have helped companies like yours achieve with a minimal investment of time and money."*

TIME: six seconds

Part 8: Close

To close this part of the sale, getting the meeting, just suggest a time to meet.

NOTE: In Cold Calling Techniques: That Really Work *by Stephan Schiffman, the author suggests closing by offering only one time option to the client. His theory is that if the time suggested is not good for them, then you may just wind up having a conversation about which time to meet—not whether or not you should meet at all. If you take this approach, have a few times prepared in advance of each call, based on the location of the client and your schedule. Don't lose your hard-won momentum at this point by fumbling through your calendar.*

EXAMPLE: *"Are you available next **Tuesday at 2:00?"***

TIME: two seconds

The whole call sounds something like this:

"Hi ____(name)____,"

"This is ME from MY COMPANY..."

"the leading ____"; "one of the ____ in all of ____...."

"I am calling because your company fits the profile of the kind of companies we help by reducing their office paper consumption by over 50 percent"

"Are you the person responsible for office waste reduction and paper consumption?"

"Oh good—(then you are the right person for me to talk to)"

"Why don't we set up a 20-minute meeting so that I can show you the kinds of savings we have helped companies like yours achieve with a minimal investment of time and money."

*"Are you available next **Tuesday at 2:00?**"*

TOTAL TIME: thirty seconds

Now practice the call until it sounds natural and spontaneous. Actors use scripts, but (most) don't sound like they do because they practice. If you practice your script, you will say the right things, say them in a highly confident manner, and get to the desired result fast. We packed a lot into 30 seconds, didn't we?

When you do this for real, you will get objections. Read Appendix C for the most common prospecting objections and some suggestions about how to manage them.

Bonus Points

Let's assume, however, that we either didn't get objections, or we did, but we handled them and now have a meeting scheduled. Here are some other important things that you can do to help ensure the success of the meeting during the time that you are setting it up:

Clarify the need.
Ask the client if there are any special concerns regarding the type of work that you do that you should be prepared to discuss. This will help you better prepare for the meeting, start the meeting in the best way, and keep the meeting focused on an area of importance to the client from the moment you begin.

Make sure all of the decision makers are there.
Ask the client if others are involved in the decision to buy your products, and if they should be at the meeting to be able to get the information first hand, and to ask any questions that they might have.

Confirm the location of the meeting.
Unless you are 1000 percent sure, ask. No sense getting this far and being late because they did not update their website, the phone book is out of date, or they are on a campus with 30 buildings.

If you have the right reason, call with confidence (because you used your script), and stayed focused on getting the meeting and not selling in the SCORE call, then your chances for success will be higher, and the potential for "psychological damage" will be minimized.

Remember to batch your calls, track your results, and to just do it. The whole rest of your sales program will work a lot better if you systematically get the right people into the front end of your process the right way. Now you know just how to get that done.

APPENDIX C
SUGGESTED RESPONSES TO
COMMON PROSPECTING OBJECTIONS

In the last several years, I have run one specific exercise in most of the trainings, workshops, and personal coaching sessions that I have facilitated on the subject of prospecting objections. The exercise goes like this:

After working through the SCORE call script as I hope you just did in Appendix B, I ask the participant(s) to write down all of the prospecting objections they have ever heard. Prospecting objections are the objections a prospective client might offer when asked to set the meeting. In a group setting, I write down answers from the participants on a white board or a flip chart. Once the group is sure they don't know any more, I hand out a pre-printed list of common prospecting objections.

As I mentioned earlier, on only one occasion in the last several years, was there something on the board that was not on the pre-printed list, and it was extremely industry specific. Accordingly, I added the "Industry Specific" objection to the list, and have never again had an objection come up from the group that was not on my list.

Why does this matter? Well, we are talking about getting a meeting, not about making a final sale. Getting a meeting is like a mini-sale within the bigger sale, but there are fewer "moving parts" than in the bigger sale. As such, it is significant that we can anticipate almost all, if not all of the potential objections to setting a meeting. If we can anticipate them, we can prepare to address them.

One important thing to realize is that at this stage, the prospect may have little or no relationship with you. Unless you are making the call to an existing client, in which case an objection is less likely and easier to handle, no one wants to waste time, so there is an almost instinctive reflex on the part of the prospective client to throw off the meeting. Towards this end, a standard prospecting objection is usually offered by the prospect, and the unprepared salesperson is usually forced to accept it. Please believe me when I say that, if you address the first objection effectively and it goes away, it was never real to begin with—it was just a reflex. If you can find a way to address these objections with confidence and competence, you will significantly increase your conversion rate in prospecting efforts.

I have listed below the common prospecting objections and some suggested responses. (If you have suggestions of new objections or alternative responses, please visit the website of this book at www.davidmasover.com and click on the "contact us" button to tell me about it. If it is indeed something new or different, I will add it to my website, and include it in the next edition of this book, credited to you.)

One last thing: Up to this point, we have crafted a "sales personality" or a "sales philosophy" of a high integrity, information-rich expert who is not interested in wasting time such as might be the case by tricking someone into a meeting that should not happen. The objection responses below are not designed to "win" each time. Rather, they are designed to force a second consideration by the prospective client before agreeing or disagreeing to the meeting. It has to be handled in a manner that is consistent with the sales persona we will want to maintain throughout all of our sales interactions. We are only looking to rattle the reflex, not twist any arms here.

These are listed in no particular order.

Common prospecting objection: I don't have time to talk to you.

Suggested response:

"I understand, but if you did have time, would the subject be of interest to you?"

COMMENTS: This is a very common objection. The goal of our question is to neutralize their immediate issue (no time) and to try to test for interest in the absence of a time restraint. If the answer remains negative, then it is time to move on. If there is interest outside of the time constraint, then seek to find a time when the prospective client can meet with you.

Common prospecting objection: Send me something.

Suggested response:

"I would be happy to, but we have a lot of different materials. Can I ask you a few questions to help me choose the right information to send to you?"

COMMENTS: Starting out by agreeing to their request, you will disarm them. But by working to clarify what information you should send, you are clarifying their specific needs. If they respond, "Just anything about your company," then they are probably just trying to get you off the phone. If, on the other hand, you are able to discuss your various product lines or specific solutions with them, then you are qualifying them and getting information to help you set up the meeting. If the conversation starts to become too detailed, then offer to bring the material by their office, so you can show them the options and answer any questions. Guess what? You got your meeting!

Common prospecting objection: We are working with someone else.

Suggested response:

"Yes, I would expect that. The reason that I am calling now is to show you what we are doing that may be different, and may in fact compliment what you are already doing. If we can meet for about 20 minutes in your office, I can show you what you may need to know about our solution to be able to decide if it fits into what you are already doing now. Are you available Friday at 2:00?"

COMMENTS: Most people who are prospects for you already have a vendor for what you sell. The worst thing you can do is talk badly about their current vendor, talk too strongly about your product, or worst of all, ask, *"Are you happy with your current vendor?"* That question is insulting to the client. If they were not happy, they would not be using them. Remember our core philosophy that if your client is not using your product or service it is because they don't know all that there is to know about it. Your job is to help them understand that, and taking the approach above to this VERY common objection will get the client to start thinking that there may be more available in the category you offer than what he gets from his current vendor, and that meeting with you, if nothing else, is a way to learn more about it.

Common prospecting objection: We don't have that in the budget.

Suggested response:

"If you did have that in the budget, would you want to move forward with it?"

COMMENTS: If you are talking to a decision maker, and they want something, they can usually manipulate the budget to get it. The value of asking this question is that it leads you to another objection, which you can address. For example, the client will say, "No, our CEO has had a bad experience with this kind of a thing in the past." Now you are past the budget question and onto another objection to address (actually two, you should also ask about the decision maker here!). If they answer "yes" to the budget question, meaning that if it was in the budget they would buy it, then you can start talking about either how to get it into the next budget before that budget is written, or what other budget this might be able to fit into that might have cash for something like what you are selling.

Common prospecting objection: I am not the decision maker.

Suggested response:

"Thanks for letting me know that. Can you tell me who I should be speaking to about this (and can you transfer me?)"

COMMENTS: This is a no-brainer, but it is important that you get the proper name, title, and phone number, and ask that you be transferred. Many company telephone systems indicate which calls come from outside and which come from inside of the company; a call that is transferred internally is more likely to be answered than one that comes from outside. Once you get to the decision maker, start again with the SCORE call script, but your reason becomes that you talked to this other person in the company (use their name), and they suggested that the person you are talking to now is the right person to talk to about your offering.

Common prospecting objection: We do that internally.

Suggested response:

"Yes, a lot of companies that I work with now had been doing this internally when we first spoke, but over time, they came to realize that we bring a broader experience set, more focused diagnostic tools, greater accountability, and ultimately improved performance at a lower cost than their internal solution. If we can meet for about 20 minutes, I can show you some of the specific areas in which we help clients make improvements above and beyond those possible by their internal resources. Are you available Friday at 2:00?"

COMMENTS: Sometimes your toughest competition will come from inside the company; however, you have an obvious asset. The fact that your company works for a large number of companies gives you an experience base and a set of tools to solve problems that is almost certainly more robust than those of your prospective client. Find a way to demonstrate the benefits to the client of harnessing your wide breadth of experience, and get an opportunity to show these benefits in a concise and compelling way. That should get you a first meeting. People want to know what they are missing. When you get the chance, don't offend the current crew doing the work, but help them to see how working with you will get better results faster, and you may win.

(NOTE: Stephan Schiffman introduced this "feel, felt, found" objection handling format to me in his aforementioned book on cold calling.)

Common prospecting objection: This is not a good time for us.

Suggested response:

"If it were a good time, would you want to move forward?"

COMMENTS: Here again we try to isolate the objection. If it is a matter of time, and at some other time they would want to move forward, your discussion becomes about "when" not "if." It is important to understand in this case WHY it is not a good time now. Then get a date to call back when the time is better for a reason you understand and agree on with the client. Be sure to flush out any other issues that may need to be addressed, so that you don't need to fight them when the time in the future comes. If the *"now is not a good time"* objection comes up for a few follow up calls in a row, consider the fact that it may NEVER be a good time, and suggest this to the client. What do you have to lose?

Common prospecting objection: Your prices are too high.

Suggested response:

"Can you help me understand what pricing you are comparing us to?"

COMMENTS: If a prospective client brings up the price objection at the time you are trying to set a first meeting, there is some information that has not yet been exchanged. At this time, you have not talked about product and pricing, but your prospective client is making assumptions. You need to understand why they feel the way they do about your prices so that you can address those concerns.

The end of the *"compared to what?"* discussion will be most successful if you can look forward into your sales process and recognize that you will need to do a needs analysis. As such, you may say to your prospective client something like:

"We offer a lot of solutions for a variety of issues, and there are different costs associated with each specific approach. Why don't we meet for about 30 minutes in your office and talk about the details of your requirements. That will allow me to estimate the pricing, and to show you how the value we add to your project justifies the prices we charge. Are you available next Friday at 2:00?"

Common prospecting objection: We're not interested.

Suggested response:

"That's funny, some of my best clients said the same thing at this stage of the conversation, but once they learned how we can help them, they became interested, and started benefiting from the results of our system. Would you allow me 20 minutes in your office, perhaps this Friday at 2:00, to show you how we changed so many minds in such a short time?"

COMMENTS: Like the *"price is too high"* objection, this objection implies that the prospective client thinks they know more than they might really know about you and your offering. Your job is not to get flustered by this, but to try to point out this fact, in a soft way, and to suggest that with a little more information, the prospective client might be like many of your best clients today, and come to see the value of your offering. The only cost is a 20-minute meeting to get the information—and guess what—you got your meeting. In case you didn't recognize it, this is another application of the "feel, felt, found" technique.

Common prospecting objection: We don't have confidence in your company.

Suggested response:

"Oh! That's not something we hear very often at all. Could you please tell me what it is about our company that causes you some concern?

COMMENTS: You'll never get past this until you ask. Most likely, there was a previous sales effort where the price was too high, the salesperson did a bad job, or the delivery went badly. You will need to convince the client that things are different now, and that you take full responsibility for the results. Offer to meet with the client to understand his concerns more fully about how things went wrong in the past. By showing that you are truly interested in understanding the problem, and assuring them it won't happen again, you may mitigate the confidence problem. You'll still have all of the other objections to address, but you got your meeting, and addressing past issues can be considered part of either mutual qualification or needs analysis. Either way, you are now into the sales process, which is the goal of the prospecting step. You have succeeded; now see what you can do with it.

By the way, try to sound sincere in your surprise at the start of this response. A heavy sigh may signal to the prospect that you hear this a lot; that is not going to work in your favor!

Common prospecting objection: I need to think about it.

Suggested response:

"I'm not sure what issues you want to consider, but what might make sense is for us to meet for about 20 minutes to flesh out your concerns together. Are you available Friday at 2:00?"

COMMENTS: This objection can be a killer after the proposal is written, unless you handle it right. The best way to handle it in response to the proposal is the same way to handle it as a prospecting objection. The philosophy behind an effective response to this objection is that whatever the issues are, it makes more sense to address them together now, than to have the prospect think about the issues alone, and later. Suggest this in the right way, and you will probably either get your meeting, or you will find out the main thing that the prospective client is thinking about, in which case you can address that.

Common prospecting objection: We never had good results with that before.

Suggested response:

"Oh, that's not something we hear very often at all. Could you please tell me what kind of issues you have experienced in the past with this kind of an approach?

COMMENTS: As you can see from the suggested response, the approach here is the same as the "confidence" objection. Until you understand what the prospective client is concerned about specifically, you can't address it. Chances are VERY good that whatever you assume to be the root of that statement is different from what the prospective client is talking about, so clear it up. You will uncover either more objections to answer, or some areas to clarify. The best result is to show understanding and help the prospective client realize that things are different, and that you can either demonstrate these differences in a meeting, or meet to understand the problems better. Either way, you get your meeting, and are in the process working toward qualification, needs analysis, solutions, and closing.

Common prospecting objection: The "Industry Specific" objection

Suggested response: No suggestion

COMMENTS: In your industry, country, or culture, there will be some things that are not addressed here. You probably know what they are, or will discover them soon enough. Like the 12 objections listed above, know what they are, and address them with the idea that your goal is to validate the objection by isolating it, clarify to the client that your solution is a good one, and if they seem qualified, get the meeting, even if the stated reason for the meeting is to further address the objection. If they invite you in, you are moving toward a sale.

Conclusion to Appendix C

Always remember that you are an expert trying to help your prospective client solve problems. If they don't see that right away, then it is your job to help them do so. Work to get past objections gracefully and with an eye toward helping the client see how helpful you can be for them. Don't fight to get appointments. Simply help prospective clients move past pre-conceived notions and the general inclination not to add anything new to their plates. Do this by helping them to see you as a professional, and your product as a benefit to them and to their organization. Following this philosophy, as well as the suggestions in this section and in this book, will go a long way toward getting you there.

APPENDIX D
SAMPLE PROCESS-BASED SALES ACTIVITY PLAN

For your reference and benefit, I am adding this appendix so that you can see at least one example of what a completed process-based sales activity plan might look like. I have chosen to use myself as the subject here, for two reasons.

The obvious reason is that I know quite well the system that I use, so there is no need for me to make anything up, interview anyone, or guess how some other industry might work. This is what I do to sell my consulting services.

The second reason is less obvious, and far more important: I have nothing to hide. I have no problem with the idea that someone I sold to yesterday or someone who I might sell to tomorrow might see this plan. There is no trickery here. No deception. No slight of hand. The plan I execute is a way for me to ensure that time spent with a prospect is in our mutual interest; if we decide that it is, then the plan is designed to help me determine and deliver the best services possible.

In this respect, it is a source of pride. Your sales practice should be for you as well. OK—I'll get off the soapbox and get to work—here is my own process-based sales activity plan for my consulting services:

(NOTE: I have organized these as a walkthrough of the exercises from Chapters 2 through 11, which is the same work you should do in order to create your own personalized plan.)

Exercises for Chapter 2
Sales Process Step #1: Leads

My Lead Sources and Times to Use Them

Referrals
Ask for referrals from clients and prospects at key points of relationship:

- When a prospect says "no" to working together after a thorough qualification and/or needs analysis, ask if they know someone else who might benefit from my services.
- When a client agrees to work with me and we sign an agreement.
- Every six months after work is initiated, I schedule a call to check in (whether work is ongoing or not) and to ask for referrals.
- Every time I hold a seminar, call entire network to ask them to invite colleagues who can come at no charge, if invited by them.

LinkedIn and Xing (online networking groups)

- Check LinkedIn and/or Xing for one hour each week, specific time to be scheduled on Friday for the following week.
- Search under criteria of Budapest and CEO / President / Managing Director. Look for companies in industries that are business-to-business and sales intensive (e.g., software, consulting). Send standard introduction message to at least 10 new contacts per week.
- Spend one hour each week adding to network so that searches can be broader.
- Add Google widget to check LinkedIn question-and-answer section of sales and business development automatically. Ask people who I interact with there to include me in their network, and if appropriate, to consult remotely.

Chamber of Commerce (one for each major country here in Hungary)

- Every six months (Q1 and Q3), schedule a seminar through a Chamber of Commerce here in Hungary, alternating between US, British, Canadian, Italian, German, French, and Nordic.
- One to two times per month, participate in networking events or educational events from these Chambers.

(NOTE: A sample of the downloadable form for making leads "call ready" is available at www.davidmasover.com/download-forms.)

Exercises for Chapter 3
Sales Process Step #2: Prospecting

My Prospecting Methods

Seminars

Hold a seminar two times per year. Topics can be:

- How to master your sales process
- Generating more revenue from your sales force
- Sales recruiting

In each seminar, identify the following key points that apply to the subject, and pre-empt the following predictable objections:

- Why we must fully understand the issues that need fixing before we try to fix them (to set up the mini-contract diagnosis process).
- Why and how a defined sales process can improve sales performance of the individual salesperson.
- Why and how a defined sales process can improve sales performance of the organization.
- Why a selling manager is not contributing the right way and what the right contributions can do for the organization.
- Why sales recruiting should be continuous.
- Why the organization must be diagnosed before the right cure can be found.

Seminar "reason for the call":

"In the seminar, we were only able to touch on subjects at a general level. The reason I am calling you now (just after the seminar) is to see if we should meet to talk about your specific needs in detail and to see if it makes sense to consider working on them together."

Online Networking Groups
- Scan for new members in my network and expand network. Send standard email introduction at least 10 times per week.

Online networking group "reason for the call":

"I am contacting you because your profile here in LinkedIn / Xing is similar to that of several companies I have worked with here in Budapest, and I would like to meet with you at your convenience to see if perhaps I may be able to help improve sales performance at your firm as well."

Referrals
- Ask for referrals at times listed above. Schedule a referral follow-up for each client and prospect on the calendar, and as soon as the referral request is made, schedule another request for same client six months later.

Referral "reason for the call":

"I'm calling because <the person who gave me the referral by name> suggested that I contact you about my sales force improvement program. Can we meet next Wednesday at 15:00 to find out if <name> was right and, more importantly, to see if it makes sense to explore the idea of working together?"

Existing Clients
- At periodic check-in for referrals, ask how things are going, and see if there may be an opportunity for tune-ups, new hires, management consulting, and so forth.

Existing clients "reason for the call":

"Hi <client>, we haven't talked for a few months, so I wanted to check in to see how things were going."

My Prospecting Objection Personalization
I did this in Appendix C. Please rewrite my words into your own to make them sound more natural for you.

Exercises for Chapter 4
Sales Process Step #3: Qualification

My List of Prospect Qualifications

Are they the decision maker?
Questions to ask while prospecting to learn this:

- *"Who should we bring to the meeting to make sure that all of the right questions are asked and all of the right issues are raised?"*
- *"Who will participate in the decision?"*

What is the pain?
Methodology:

- Since they agreed to meet me, confirm when we meet that they want to improve sales, then ask them what they think is wrong. Probe, suggest trial solutions, and keep asking "what else?"
- Once the list seems done, read back their concerns and ask them if we missed anything.
- Rephrase the list as at least four questions we need to answer before understanding how to fix the problems we identified, for example:

"Well, to answer these questions and fix these issues, it sounds like we need to better understand the following:

1. *Which of your salespeople have the right skills to take your company to the next level?*
2. *Is your sales manager doing everything possible to help move the organization forward?*
3. *Do you have the right sales process in place to support optimal growth?*
4. *Are you measuring the right metrics?"*

- If the client agrees to the questions, then close the mini-contract for a diagnosis.

- If the situation is so bad, and the problems are crystal clear, suggest process development, training, and coaching without diagnosis.
- If no sales organization exists, then suggest process development, manager development, and recruiting process development and deployment.
- There may be some other opportunity to work together, but these three seem to capture over 90 percent of the situations I currently face. The other 10 percent can be dealt with on the fly.

Budget.

- As we are in our first meeting, and we have identified a tentative plan of action, it is possible now to either clearly specify or estimate the cost of a program of working together, especially if it is one of the common ways I work with clients. I carry a printed price sheet of common services I provide. This can be a good time to take it out and walk the client through the services that might apply to their needs and the costs involved.
- With or without a price sheet, identify with the client the steps that need to be taken to address the immediately identified problems, and tell the client what the cost is.
- If they agree that this is the appropriate course of action, then close the deal, and go write it up in a proposal.

Exercises for Chapter 5
Process Shortcut #1: The Mini-Contract

- The mini-contract, if applicable, is the diagnostic process that I use with sales organizations. This diagnostic process has a fixed cost per number of participants. If the pain identified is verified by the issues and questions that must be answered to address them, then I immediately close with the diagnosis based on the justification that we can't fix what we don't fully understand, so let's first fully understand the problems using the diagnosis process, then decide after the diagnosis what the best course of action is to fix the problems we identify.

- If the solution seems to be a process program or a recruiting program, then I have enough information to close the full deal at this time.
- If the solution is in the 10 percent category of "wow, this is new," then we play it by ear, close now if possible or at least specify the elements in the proposal and the estimated cost, even before a deeper needs analysis, which will be charged for as consulting.

Exercises for Chapter 6
Sales Process Step #4: Needs Analysis

What Do I Need to Know

- In the mini-contract method I use, I break needs analysis into two parts.

  □ The first is described in the Qualification and Mini-Contract sections. These relate to identifying the issues that I need to understand before fully solving the client's problem. Specifically, they are the questions that need to be answered before we can understand the broader question of what is not working well in the sales organization so that we can then fix it. We answer these questions with a detailed diagnosis, my mini-contract, which is a detailed form of needs analysis.

  □ The second is the presentation of the results of the diagnosis. This is a formal needs analysis review based on the findings of the diagnostic process, which allows me to close on training, coaching, and consulting business.

- If the client's needs are something other than organizational level modification and improvement, then the needs analysis is not mini-contract based, and more traditional.
- When the end result is a process development and/or a sales recruiting program, my needs analysis process simply needs to identify current frustrations and/or lack of results in sales or

sales management to support these probable causes and cures. Answers to the "pain" questions below and their follow-up questions can lead me to the right direction from among these common options.

My List of Sources of Pain to Find

Examples of the kind of pain I work to identify with my prospective clients include:

- Salespeople are not meeting their numbers.
- Salespeople are not opening enough new business.
- Salespeople are not prospecting.
- Salespeople are writing too many proposals that do not turn into business.
- Company is not growing sales revenue.
- Sales manager is selling and not managing.
- Only a small number of salespeople are performing well.

My Map for Bringing Pain to the Surface of the Needs Analysis Conversation

(NOTE: Please see Chapter 7 for an illustration of how I bring these points together for my business and how I manage the needs analysis conversation to allow me to address these points in a way to get me the information I need to set up a successful close.)

My List of Company, Product and Industry Specific Issues

- Is the sales manager role also being played by the sales or company executive?
- Is the sales or company executive decision maker willing to make changes that may include replacement of the sales manager?
- Is the sales or company executive decision maker willing to make changes that may include replacement of some of the salespeople?

- Is the sales or company executive decision maker willing to make changes to the sales process, company organization, compensation, work allocation, and other issues that may need to be reviewed in order to optimize sales performance?

My Closing Question for Needs Analysis

"So, these are the issues that we have identified so far: (list issues). Have we missed anything?"

Exercises for Chapter 7
Process Shortcut #2: The Professional Close

My Mental Map of the Steps Leading Up to a Professional Close

(NOTE: Please review Chapters 3 through 7 for the steps to take to lead to an early professional close.)

My Professional Close Questions

Question #1:

"So, we agreed that these are the issues we need to address (restate the list). Does that all sound right?"

Question #2A (after needs analysis with trial solutions):

"So as we were discussing the issues (in the needs analysis phase), I suggested some tentative solutions. Can we review them?"

(Review trial solutions)

"Generally speaking, does that sound like it will solve the problem within your budget, in a way that you think my firm can deliver the solution?"

Question #2B (after presentation of solution):

"So, does the solution I have presented solve the problem within your budget, in a way that you think my firm can deliver the solution?"

Question #3:
> *"Great—so when can we get started?"*

My Pre-Proposal Check List

- Elements of scope of work.
- Associated cost per item or per unit of work (e.g., per hour).
- Delivery dates for initial elements.
- Steps to completion of agreement after proposal is delivered.

Exercises for Chapter 8
Sales Process Step #5: Presenting the Solution

My script for the End of the Needs Analysis and Pre-Proposal Stage

(NOTE: Please see exercises for Chapter 7. I have front loaded this to that stage of the process.)

Exercises for Chapter 9
Sales Process Step #6: Objections and Negotiations

(NOTE: Please review Chapter 9 for my approaches to the exercises and how you can practice them in your own sales situations.)

Exercises for Chapter 10
Sales Process Step #7: Closing the Deal

My Closing Question:
> *"Great, sounds like we have a plan! I'll write this up as a proposal and send you an invoice for the deposit this evening, so we can get started on schedule."*

Exercises for Chapter 11
Developing Your Process-Based Sales Activity Plan

Lead Sources

Referrals

Schedule on a contact-by-contact basis at points listed in exercises for Chapter 2 here in the Chapter 11 summary including:

- After a "no".
- After a "yes".
- Every six months afterwards.
- Twice a year to ask for names for seminars.

LinkedIn

- Schedule one hour per week to search for new leads.
- Send 10 new contacts per week to new leads.
- Schedule one hour each week to broaden network.
- Answer applicable questions as they come in via Google Widget; check daily.

Chambers of Commerce of various countries

- Schedule a seminar every six months with one Chamber.
- Participate in at least one, preferably two networking events each month in different Chambers, so that all are visited at least once every three months.

Prospecting Methods

Seminars

- Hold one every six months, set up to make SCORE call after each and track on opportunity tracker.

Online Networking Groups

- See metrics above under leads (LinkedIn).

Referrals and Existing Clients
- See metrics above under leads.

My Opportunity Tracking System

(NOTE: Please see www.davidmasover.com/download-forms for a download-able sample of the simple Excel-based tracking system that I use for tracking opportunities.)

My Database Purging Meeting

- I have no inactive names in my client database, since I have already done this work.
- My contacts are classified and scheduled on an ongoing basis as follows:

    1. Active: They have something scheduled in my calendar.
    2. Non-Active / Marketing: There is no perceived potential, but I send them periodic marketing updates (stored in "marketing" database).
    3. Non-Active: There is no scheduled activity and no contact (stored in "inactive" database).

31417479R00126

Made in the USA
Lexington, KY
11 April 2014